T0316468

English Literature for Schools

Selections from the Paston Letters

The Paston Letters

A Selection Illustrating English Social Life in the Fifteenth Century

Edited with Introduction and Notes

by

M. D. JONES

Cambridge:
at the University Press
1909

CAMBRIDGE
UNIVERSITY PRESS

University Printing House, Cambridge CB2 8BS, United Kingdom

Cambridge University Press is part of the University of Cambridge.

It furthers the University's mission by disseminating knowledge in the pursuit of
education, learning and research at the highest international levels of excellence.

www.cambridge.org
Information on this title: www.cambridge.org/9781107453685

© Cambridge University Press 1909

First published 1909
First paperback edition 2014

A catalogue record for this publication is available from the British Library

ISBN 978-1-107-45368-5 Paperback

PREFACE

THIS volume contains a small proportion of the large number of " Paston Letters," which were for the most part written by various members of the family of Paston, in Norfolk, during the reigns of Henry the Sixth, Edward the Fourth, Richard the Third and Henry the Seventh.

The intention of this selection from the mass of the Letters is to illustrate as far as possible the daily life and the customs of the time in which they were written. So many vivid and homely pictures are seen through their medium, that it is hoped that the reader will be attracted by the familiar detail thus presented to search further in the mine of wealth represented by complete editions of the Letters.

The dates of the Letters selected are from 1440 to 1485, and they are placed in chronological order mainly according to the arrangement in Fenn's edition. The spelling is modernised except in the case of obsolete words, of which an explanation will be found in the notes at the end of the book.

A pedigree of the Paston family has also been added, with notes on the more important members; it is hoped that this will be found useful in identifying the individual writers.

M. D. J.

CHINGFORD,
8 *November* 1909

CONTENTS

CONTENTS

CONTENTS

INTRODUCTION

THE Paston Letters have an exceptional and singular value to the historian, for they throw light upon a period of English history which is most barren of material. During the turbulent times of the Wars of the Roses, there is a great dearth of records, and the wealth of information which the Letters give us is the more precious, for, as Sir John Fenn—who was the first to bring out an edition of the Letters—says in speaking of that troublous age, " battle and executions alone mark out to the historian his path...and his most trusty guide is the genealogist, who, recording the years in which such or such of the great nobility were beheaded, ascertains the dates of the various revolutions."

But it is not only as history that the Letters are of interest to us in the twentieth century, but because they give us unrivalled pictures of the intimate life of English country gentlefolk of more than five hundred years ago. As Hallam says, in his *Literature of Europe*—" The Paston Letters are...an important testimony to the progressive condition of society, and come in as a precious link in the chain of the moral history of England, which they alone in this period supply." We may, if we

will, go hand in hand with our imagination and enter
in upon tales not only of high politics and warlike
jousts and assaults, but upon descriptions of the life
of a Norfolk family, and learn of the manner of
their sports and of their Christmas merrymakings,
the cost of their household linen and a hundred
details having each its special interest.   Or again,
we may read of the errands in London of Agnes
Paston, then on her way to see her son Clement
and his tutor, and Elizabeth, her daughter who was
living with Lady Pole.   The women of the time
were no idle fine ladies, if we are to take the writers
and readers of these Letters as an example.
Margaret Paston was as ready to superintend the
defence of her house against attack in war-time, in
the absence of her husband, and to deal with legal
difficulties as they arose, as to give directions for
the replenishing of her store room and the purchase
of frieze for new gowns for her children.   Many
of the Letters are full of interest of this kind, and
the glimpse we get of a boy's life at Eton in those
days, and his Lenten fare there, is particularly
attractive.   As Fenn adds in the Preface to his
edition, " The principal satisfaction of the reader
will arise from two sources.   He will hear the
events of the moment from persons living at the
time, and will see the manners and usages of
that age, painted in the most familiar language,
undisguised and unadorned."

The first edition of the Letters was published in
1787 by Fenn in two quarto volumes.   He dedicated
the work to the King, George III, under the title
" Original letters, written during the reigns of
Henry VI, Edward IV and Richard III by various
persons of Rank and Consequence; containing many
curious anecdotes, relative to that turbulent and
bloody but hitherto dark, Period of our History; and

elucidating, not only Public matters of State, but likewise the Private Manners of the Age; digested in Chronological Order, with Notes, historical and explanatory; and authenticated by Engravings of Autographs, Fac-Similes, Paper-Marks and Seals."

The publication of the Letters was most successful and was warmly welcomed by Sir Horace Walpole. Encouraged by this reception, Fenn published a third and a fourth volume in 1789 and in 1823 a fifth volume was issued by his nephew, Mr William Frere, Sergeant at Law, from the matter left ready for publication by Fenn on his death in 1794. This edition has on the one page an exact transcript of the Letters as they read in the manuscript and on the opposite page a translation by Fenn in the orthography of his day. In 1840 a selection of the Letters with present day spelling was brought out by H. Ramsay and published in Knight's Miscellanies, and was included in Bohn's Antiquarian Classics in 1849. In 1872 Mr James Gairdner issued three volumes of the Letters as reproductions of the manuscripts. These were reprinted in 1900 and in 1904 a six-volume edition was issued completing his standard and invaluable work.

The history of the manuscripts of the Letters is so strange, that a short account of the vicissitudes through which they passed before they were finally printed and published may prove of interest. For several generations the Letters had been preserved as an heirloom in the Paston family itself, until they came into the possession of a great antiquary and collector, Mr Peter Le Neve, who was Norroy King at Arms (1661–1729), and from him they passed to a Mr Thomas Martin, who had married his widow. Martin's various collections, and among them the Letters, were purchased by Mr Worth, an apothecary and chemist at Diss in Norfolk who intended to arrange and dispose of them. He, however, died in 1774 before completing the sale of all the books and collections, and in the same year the manuscript of the Letters was purchased by Mr (afterwards Sir John) Fenn. After this a curious fate seemed to dog the manuscript. Fenn presented the originals of his first two volumes on their publication to George III, after which, as Mr Gairdner says, all trace of them was lost until they came to light twenty years ago (1889) at Orwell Park, Suffolk, and they are now in the possession of Mr E. G. Pretyman, M.P.

The manuscripts of volumes three, four and five were also missing for long, and Mr Gairdner gives us the subsequent history of these also. The MS. of volume five was discovered in 1865 in Mr Frere's own house, and is now in the British Museum. The originals of volumes three and four were at length discovered at Roydon House, Norfolk; they were offered for sale in 1888 at Christie's and were acquired by the British Museum authorities in 1896. This is, in brief, the history of the main collection of the Letters.

Speaking of their form and size, as they appear originally, Fenn tells us that they are for the most part neatly folded in different shapes, from three to four inches in length, and from one and a half to three inches in breadth, having either a hole cut by a knife, and a piece of paper put through it, or threads drawn through by a needle, and brought under the seal by which they were fastened.

M. D. J.

8 *November* 1909.

PEDIGREE OF THE PASTON FAMILY

*Sir WILLIAM PASTON born 1378, died 1444. Called the Good Judge.

=

†AGNES, daughter of Sir Thomas Berry, died 1479. Both she and her husband are buried in Norwich Cathedral.

---

*†JOHN PASTON, Esquire, born 1420, married before 1440. Estates seized by Edward IV; imprisoned in the Fleet; died 1466. Buried at Bromholm Priory.

=

*†MARGARET, d. of John Mauteby, Esq. Her will proved in 1484.

*EDMUND PASTON at Clifford's Inn in 1444.

WILLIAM PASTON

CLEMENT PASTON b. 1442. At London under care of Master Greenfield 1457.

ELIZABETH PASTON = Robert Poynings. She lived with Lady Pole in 1457.

---

*†Sir JOHN PASTON, Knight, born about 1440; a brave soldier; in the French wars; died unmarried in 1479.

*†JOHN PASTON, Esquire, appears to have been brought up in the family of Duke of Norfolk; in French wars; attended Princess Margaret to Bruges in 1468; heir to his brother 1479; High Sheriff of Norfolk 1485; died 1503.

=

†MARGERY, d. of Sir Thomas Brews; married 1477; died 1495.

†WILLIAM PASTON at Eton 1467.

CLEMENT PASTON

WALTER PASTON took a degree and died at Oxford 1479.

*EDMUND PASTON in the garrison at Calais 1473; died about 1504.

ANNE PASTON = William Velverton.

MARGERY PASTON = Richard Calle.

---

* Letters addressed to.　　†Letters written by.　　* Letters written by.

SELECTIONS FROM THE PASTON LETTERS

I. *To my worshipful husband, William Paston, be this letter taken.*

(About 1440)

Dear husband, I recommend me to you, etc. Blessed be God I send you good tidings of the coming and the bringing home of the gentlewoman that ye weeten of from Reedham this same night, according to appointment that ye made there for yourself.

And as for the first acquaintance between John Paston and the said gentlewoman, she made him gentle cheer in gentle wise, and said he was verily your son; and so I hope there shall need no great treaty between them.

The parson of Stockton told me if ye would buy her a gown, her mother would give thereto a goodly fur. The gown needeth to be had; and of colour it would be a goodly blue, or else a bright sanguine.

I pray you to buy for me two pipes of gold. Your stews do well. The Holy Trinity have you in governance. Written at Paston in haste the Wednesday next after "Deus qui errantibus" for default of a good secretary etc.

Yours,

AGNES PASTON.

II. *To my right worshipful husband, John Paston,
dwelling in the Inner Temple at London, in
haste.*

(1443)

Right Worshipful husband, I recommend me to
you, desiring heartily to hear of your welfare, thanking
God for your amending of the great disease that ye
have had; and I thank you for the letter that ye sent
me, for by my troth my mother and I were nought in
heart's ease from the time that we wist of your sickness, till we wist verily of your amending. My mother
behested another image of wax of the weight of you,
to our Lady of Walsingham, and she sent four nobles
to the four orders of friars at Norwich to pray for you,
and I have behested to go on a pilgrimage to Walsingham and to St Leonard's for you; by my troth I had
never so heavy a season as I had from the time that I
wist of your sickness, till I wist of your amending, and
yet my heart is in no great ease nor shall be, till I
weet that ye be very whole. Your father and mine
was this day sev'night at Beccles, for a matter of the
Prior of Bromholm, and he lay at Gelderstone that
night, and was there till it was nine of the clock and
the other day. And I sent thither for a gown, and
my mother said that I should none have then till I
had been there anon, and so they could none get.

My father Garneys sent me word that he should
have been here the next week and my emme also, and
play them here with their hawks, and they should
have me home with them, and so God help me, I shall
excuse myself from going thither if I may, for I
suppose that I shall more readily have tidings from
you here than I should have there. I shall send my
mother a token that she took me, for I suppose the
time is come that I should send it her, if I keep the
behest that I have made; I suppose I have told you
what it was. I pray you heartily that ye will vouchsafe
to send me a letter as hastily as ye may, if writing be
none disease to you, and that ye will vouchsafe to

send me word how your sore do. If I might have had
my will, I should have seen you ere this time; I would
ye were at home, if it were your ease, and your sore
might be as well looked to here as it is there ye be
now, lever than a gown, though it were of scarlet. I
pray you if your sore be whole so that ye may endure
to ride when my father comes to London, that ye will
ask leave and come home when the horse should be
sent home again, for I hope ye shall be kept as ten-
derly here as ye be at London. I may none leisure
have to do write half a quarter so much as I should
say to you if I might speak with you. I shall send you
another letter as hastily as I may. I thank you that
ye would vouchsafe to remember my girdle, and that
ye would write to me at the time, for I suppose that
writing was none ease to you. Almighty God have
you in his keeping, and send you health. Written at
Oxnead, in right great haste, on St Michael's even.

Yours,

M. PASTON.

My mother greet you well, and sendeth you God's
blessing and hers; and she prayeth you, and I pray
you also, that ye be well dieted of meat and drink, for
that is the greatest help that ye may have now to your
healthward. Your son fareth well, blessed be God.

III. *To my well-beloved son, John Paston,
be this delivered in haste.*

(About 1444)

Son, I greet you well, and let you weet that forasmuch as your brother Clement letteth me weet that
ye desire faithfully my blessing; that blessing that I
prayed your father to give you the last day that ever
he spake, and the blessing of all saints under heaven,
and mine mote come to you all days and times; and
think verily none other but that ye have it, and shall
have it, with that that I find you kind and willing to

1—2

the weal of your father's soul, and to the welfare of your brethren. By my counsel, dispose yourself as much as ye may to have less to do in the world: your father said, "In little business lieth much rest." This world is but a thoroughfare, and full of woe, and when we depart therefrom, right nought bear with us, but our good deeds and ill. And there knoweth no man how soon God will clepe him, and therefore it is good for every creature to be ready. Whom God visiteth, him he loveth.

And as for your brethren they will I know certainly labour all that in them lyeth for you. Our Lord have you in his blessed keeping, body and soul. Written at Norwich, the 29th day of October.

By your mother,

AGNES PASTON.

IV. *To John Paston, dwelling in the Temple at London, be this letter delivered in haste.*

(About 1444)

I greet you well, and let you weet, that on the Sunday before St Edmund, after evensong, Agnes Ball came to me to my closet and bade me good even, and Clement Spicer with her; and I asked him what he would. And he asked me why I had stopped in the king's way; and I said to him I stopped no way but mine own, and asked him why he had sold my land to John Ball and he swore he was never accorded with your father, and I told him if his father had done as he did, he would have been ashamed to have said as he said; and all that time Waryn Herman leaned over the park close and listened to what we said, and said that the change was a rewly change, for the town was undo thereby, and is the worse by a hundred pounds. And I told him it was no courtesy to meddle him in a matter but if he were called to council; and proudly going forth with me in the church, he said the stopping of the

way should cost me twenty nobles and yet it should
be down again.   And I let him weet, he that put it
down should pay therefore.

Also he said that it was well done that I set men
to work to owl many while I was here, but in the end
I shall lose my cost.   Then he asked me why I had
(taken) away his hay at Walsham, saying to me he
would he had wist it, when it was carried, and he
should a letted it; and I told him it was mine own
ground, and for mine own I would hold it; and
he bade me take four acres and go no further, and
thus churtly he departed from me in the churchyard;
and since I spake with a certain man, and asked him
if he heard ought say why the dinner was made at
Norfolk's house, and he told me (he) heard say that
certain men had sent to London to get a commission
out of the Chancery to put down again the wall and
the dyke.

I received your letter by Robert Repps this day,
after this letter (was) written thus far.   I have read
it, but I can give you none answer more than I have
written, save the wife of Harman hath the name of our
Lady, whose blessing ye have and mine.   Written at
Paston, on the day after St Edmond.

By your mother,

Agnes Paston.

V.   *To Edmund Paston of Clifford's Inn in
London, be this letter taken.*

(1444)

To mine well-beloved son.   I greet you well, and
advise you to think once of the day of your father's
counsel to learn the law, for he said many times that
whosoever should dwell at Paston, should have need
to con defend himself.

The Vicar of Paston and your father in Lent last
was, were thorough and accorded, and doles set how

broad the way should be, and now he hath pulled up
the doles and saith he will make a ditch from the
corner of his wall, right over the way to the new ditch
of the great close.   And there is a man in Trunch
hight Palmer too, that had of your father certain lands
in Trunch over seven years or eight years agone, for
corn, and truly hath paid all the years; and now he
hath suffered the corn to be withset for eight shillings
of rent to Gimmingham, which your father paid never.
Geoffry asked Palmer why the rent was not asked in
mine husband's time and Palmer said, for he was a
great man, and a wise man of the law, and that was
the cause men would not ask him the rent.

I send you the names of the men, that cast down
the pit that was (in) Genney's Close, written in a bill
closed in this letter.

I send you not this letter to make you weary of
Paston, for I live in hope, and ye will learn that they
shall be made weary of their work, for in good faith
I dare well say it was your father's last will to have
done right well to that place, and that can I shew of
good proof though men would say nay.   God make
you right a good man, and send God's blessing and
mine.   Written in haste at Norwich, the Thursday
after Candlemas day.

Weet of your brother John how many joists will
serve the parlour and the Chapel at Paston and what
length they must be, and what breadth and thickness
they must be, for your father's will was, as I ween
verily, that they should be nine inches one way, and
seven another way, and purvey therefore that they
may be squared there, and sent hither, for here can
none such be had in this country; and say to your
brother John it were well done to think on Stansted
Church; and I pray you to send me tidings from beyond
sea, for here they are afraid to tell such as be reported.

By your mother,

AGNES PASTON.

VI. *To my trusty and well-beloved friend, Sir Thomas Howys, parson of Castlecomb.*

(1450)

Trusty and well-beloved friend, I greet you well.... And I pray you send me word who dare be so hardy to kick against you in my right. And say (to) them on my half that they shall be quyt as far as law and reason will. And if they will not dread nor obey that, then they shall be quyt by Blackbeard or Whitebeard, is to say by God or the Devil. And therefore I charge you send me word whether such as have been mine adversaries before this time continue still in their wilfulness etc.

Item, I hear ofttimes many strange reports of the demenys of the governance of my place at Caister, and other places, as in my chatell approving, in my wines, the keeping of my wardrobe and clothes, the avail of my conies at Hellesdon etc. and approvement of my lands; praying you heartily as my full trust is in you to help reform it, and that ye suffer no vicious man at my place of Caister abide, but well governed and diligent, as ye will answer to it.

Almighty God keep you. Written at London, the 27th day of May, in the 28th year of the reign of King Henry VI.

JOHN FASTOLF, Knight.

VII. *To my right worshipful husband, John Paston, be this delivered in haste.*

(1451)

*   *   *   *   *   *   *   *

I was at Topp's at dinner on Saint Peter's day, there my Lady Felbrigg and other gentlewomen desired to have had you there; they said they should all have been the merrier if you had been there. My cousin Topps hath much care till she hears good tidings of her brother's matter; she told me that they should keep a day on Monday next coming betwixt her brother and Sir Andrew Hugard and Wyndham. I pray you send me word how they speed and how ye speed in your own matters also.

Also I pray you heartily that ye will send me a pot of treacle in haste, for I have been right evil at ease, and your daughter both, since that ye yeden hence, and one of the tallest young men of this parish lieth sick, and hath a great myrr, how he shall do, God knoweth.

I have sent my uncle Berney the pot with treacle that ye did buy for him; mine aunt recommendeth her to you and prayeth you to do for her as the bill maketh mention of, that I send you with this letter, and as ye think best to do therein. Sir Harry Inglose is passed to God this night, whose soul God assoil; and was carried forth this day at nine of the clock to Saint Faith's and there shall be buried.

If ye desire to buy any of his stuff, I pray you send me word thereof in haste, and I shall speak to Robert Inglos, and to Wichingham thereof; I suppose they be executors.

The blessed Trinity have you in his keeping. Written at Norwich in haste on the Thursday next after Saint Peter.

I pray you trust not to the sheriff for no fair language.

Yours,

Margaret Paston.

VIII. *To my right worshipful master, John Paston, be this delivered in haste.*

(1452)

Right worshipful husband, I recommend me to you, praying you to weet etc....

As for tidings, the Queen came into this town on Tuesday last past after noon, and abode here till it was Thursday three after noon; and she sent after my cousin Elizabeth Clere by Sharinborn to come to her, and she durst not disobey her commandment, and came to her; and when she came in the Queen's presence, the Queen made right much of her, and desired her to have an husband, the which ye shall know of hereafter; but as for that, he is never nearer than he was before. The Queen was right well pleased with her answer and reported of her in the best wise and saith, by her troth, she saw no gentlewoman since she came into Norfolk that she liked better than she doth her.

Blake, the bailey of Swaffham was here with the King's brother and he came to me, weening that ye had been at home; and said that the King's brother desired him that he should pray you in his name to come to him, for he would right fain that ye had come to him, if ye had been at home. And he told me, that he wist well that he should send for you, when he came to London, both for Cossey and other things.

I pray you that ye will do your cost on me against Whitsuntide that I may have something for my neck. When the Queen was here, I borrowed my cousin Elizabeth Clere's device for I durst not for shame go with my beads among so many fresh gentlewomen as here were at that time.

The blessed Trinity have you in his keeping. Written at Norwich on the Friday next before Saint George.

By yours,

Margaret Paston.

IX. *To my right worshipful husband, John
Paston, be this delivered in haste.*

(1452)

Right worshipful husband, I commend me to you,
I pray you that ye will do buy two dozen trenchers,
for I can none get in this town. Also I pray you that
ye will send me a book with chardeqweyns that I may
have of in the morning, for the air be not wholesome
in this town, therefore I pray you heartily let John
Suffield bring it home with him.

No more, but the blessed Trinity have you in his
keeping and send you good speed in all your matters.
Written on St Leonard's even.

My uncle Philip commends him to you, and he hath
been so sick since I came to Reedham, that I wend
he should never have escaped it, nor not is like to do,
but if he have ready help, and therefore he shall into
Suffolk this next week, to mine aunt, for there is a
good physician, and he shall look to him.

My Lady Hastyngs told me that Heydon hath
spoken to Jeffrey Boleyn of London, and is agreed
with him that he should bargain with Sir John
Fastolf to buy the manor of Blickling, as it were
for himself, and if Boleyn buy it, in truth Heydon
shall have it.

I came to Norwich on Soulmass Day.

Yours,
Margaret Paston.

X. *To my well-beloved son, John Paston.*

(1453)

Son, I greet you well, and send you God's blessing
and mine, and let you weet that Robert Hill came
homeward by Orwellbury, and Gurney telled him he,
had been at London for money and could not speeden,
and behested Robert that he should send me money
by you. I pray you forget it not as ye come homeward,
and speak sadly for another farmer.

And as for tidings, Philip Berney is passed to God

on Monday last past, with the greatest pain that ever I saw man; and on Tuesday Sir John Heveningham yede to his church and heard three masses and came home again never merrier, and said to his wife that he would go say a little devotion in his garden, and then he would dine, and forthwith he felt a fainting in his legs, and sydd down. This was at nine of the clock and he was dead ere noon.

My cousin Clere prays you that ye let no man see her letter, which is ensealed under my seal. I pray you that ye will pay your brother William for four ounces and a half of silk, as he paid, which he sent me by William Taverner, and bring with you a quarter of an ounce even like of the same that I send you closed in this letter, and say your brother William, that his horse hath one farcy and great running sores in his legs. God have you in his keeping. Written at Norwich, on Saint Thomas's even, in great haste.

By your mother,

AGNES PASTON.

XI. *To my right worshipful husband, John Paston, be this delivered in haste.*

(1454)

Right worshipful husband, I recommend me to you, beseeching you that ye be not displeased with me, though my simpleness caused you for to be displeased with me. By my troth it is not my will neither to do nor say that which should cause you for to be displeased, and if I have done (it), I am sorry thereof and will amend it; whereof I beseech you to forgive me, and that ye bear none heaviness in your heart against me, for your displeasure should be too heavy to me to endure with.

I send you the roll that ye sent for, ensealed by the bringer hereof; it was found in your trussing coffer. As for herring, I have bought a horseload for 4/6d. I can get none eels yet; as for bever there is promised me some, but I might not get it yet. I sent to Joan Petche to have an answer for the windows, for she might not come to me, and she sent me word that she had spoken thereof to Thomas Ingham, and he said that he should speak with you himself, and he should accord with you well enough, and he said to her it was not her part to desire of him to stop the lights; and also he said it was not his part to do it, because the place is his but for years.

And as for all other errands that you have commanded to be done, they shall be done as soon as they may be done. The blessed Trinity have you in his keeping. Written at Norwich, on the Monday next after Saint Edward.

Yours,

MARGARET PASTON.

XII. *To my right worshipful husband, John Paston, be this delivered in haste.*

(1455 or 1460)

Right worshipful husband, I recommend me unto you. Pleaseth you to weet that mine Aunt Moundford hath desired me to write to you, beseeching you that ye will vouchsafe to chevise for her at London twenty marks for to be paid to Master Ponyngs, either on Saturday or Sunday, which shall be St Andrew's day, in discharging of them that be bounden to Master Ponyngs of the said twenty marks for the wardship of her daughter, the which twenty marks she hath delivered to me in gold for you to have at your coming home, for she dare not adventure her money to be brought up to London for fear of robbing, for it is said here that there goeth many thieves betwixt this and London, which causeth her to beseech you to content the said money in discharging of the matter and of them that be bounden, for she would for no good that the day were broken. And she thanketh you heartily for the great labour and business that ye have had in that matter, and in all others touching her and hers, wherefore she saith she is ever bound to be your beadswoman, and ever will be while she liveth.

My cousin, her son, and his wife recommendeth them unto you, beseeching you that ye will vouchsafe to be their good master, as ye have aforetime; for they be informed that Daniel is come to Rising Castle, and his men make their boast that their master shall be again at Brayston within short time.

Furthermore, as for the matter that my son wrote to me for the box whereon was written *False Carte Sproute*, that I should inquire of William Worcester where it were; the said William was not at home since that I had his letter, but as soon as he cometh home I shall inquire of him, and send you an answer.

As touching for your liveries, there can none be gotten here of that colour that ye would have of, neither murrey, nor blue, nor good russet, underneath 3s. the yard at the lowest price, and yet is there not enough of one cloth and colour to serve you; and as for to be purveyed in Suffolk, it will not be purveyed now against the time, without they had had warning at Michaelmas, as I am informed: and the blessed Trinity have you in his keeping. Written at Norwich, on St Katherine's day.

By your

Margaret Paston.

XIII. *Errands to London of Agnes Paston, the 28th day of January*, 1457, *the year of King Henry VI, the 36th.*

(1457)

To pray Greenfield to send me faithfully word, by writing, how Clement Paston hath done his endeavour in learning. And if he hath not done well, nor will not amend, pray him that he will truly belash him, till he will amend, and so did the last master, and the best that ever he had at Cambridge. And say (to) Greenfield that if he will take upon him to bring him into good rule and learning, that I may verily know he doth his endeavour, I will give him ten marks for his labour, for I had lever he were fairly buried than lost for default

Item, to see how many gowns Clement hath; and they that be bare, let them be raised. He hath a short green gown, and a short musterdevelers gown, (which) were never raised, and a short blue gown that was raised, and made of a side gown, when I was last at London. And a side russet gown, furred with beaver, was made this time two years; and a side murrey gown was made this time twelvemonth.

Item, to do make me six spoons, of eight ounces of Troy weight, wellfashioned and double-gilt.

And say (to) Elizabeth Paston, that she must use herself to work readily as other gentlewomen do, and somewhat to help herself therewith.

Item, to pay the Lady Pole 26 shillings and 8*d*. for her board.

And if Greenfield have done his devoir well to Clement, or will do his devoir, give him the noble.

AGNES PASTON.

XIV. *To my right worshipful husband, John Paston.*

(Before 1459)

Right worshipful husband, I recommend me to you, and pray you to get some crossbows and wyndacs to bind them with, and quarrels, for your houses here be so low that there may none man shoot out with no long bow, though we had never so much need.

I suppose ye should have such things of Sir John Fastolf if ye would send to him; and also I would ye should get two or three short poleaxes to keep with(in) doors, and as many jackets, and ye may.

Partrich and his fellowship are sore afraid that ye would enter again upon them and they have made great ordinance within the house, and it is told me they have made bars to bar the doors crosswise, and they have made wickets on every quarter of the house to shoot out at, both with bows and with hand-guns;

and the holes that be made for hand-guns, they be scarce knee high from the plancher, and of such holes be made five, there can none man shoot out at them with no hand-bows.

    *   *   *   *   *   *   *   *

I pray you that ye will vouchsafe to do buy for me one pound of almonds and one pound of sugar, and that ye will do buy some frieze to make of your children's gowns; ye shall have best cheap and best choice of Hays's wife, as it is told me. And that ye will buy a yard of broad cloth of black for one hood for me of 44*d.* or four shillings a yard, for there is neither good cloth nor good frieze in this town. As for the children's gowns, and I have them I will do them maken.

The Trinity have you in his keeping, and send you good speed in all your matters.

MARGARET PASTON.

XV. *Unto my right worshipful cousin, Margaret Paston, this letter be delivered in haste.*

(1458)

Right worshipful, and my most best beloved mistress and cousin, I recommend me unto you as lowly as I may, evermore desiring to hear of your good welfare, the which I beseech Almighty Jesu to preserve you, and keep you to his pleasure, and to your gracious heart's desire.

And if it please you to hear of my welfare, I was in good hele at the making of this letter, blessed be God; praying you, that it please you for to send me word, if my father were at Norwich with you at this Trinity Mass or no, and how the matter doth between my mistress Blanch Witchingham and me, and if ye suppose that it shall be brought about or no, and how ye feel my father, if he be well willing thereto or no, praying you lowly that I may be recommended lowly unto my mistress, Arblaster's wife, and unto my mistress Blanch her daughter specially.

Right worshipful cousin, if it please you to hear of such tidings as we have here, the basset of Burgundy shall come to Calais the Saturday after Corpus Christi day, as men say five hundred horse of them.

Moreover, on Trinity Sunday in the morning, came tidings unto my Lord of Warwick, that there were 28 sail of Spaniards on the sea, and whereof there was sixteen great ships of forecastle; and then my Lord went, and manned five ships of forecastle and three carvells and four spynnes; and on the Monday, in the morning after Trinity Sunday, we met together before Calais at four at the clock in the morning, and fought together till ten at the clock; and there we took six of their ships, and they slew of our men about four score, and hurt a two hundred of us right sore, and there were slain on their part about a hundred and twenty, and hurt a five hundred of them.

And happed me, at the first aboarding of us, we took a ship of three hundred ton, and I was left therein, and twenty three men with me; and they fought so sore that our men were fain to leave them, and then come they and aboarded the ship that I was in, and there I was taken, and was prisoner with them six hours, and was delivered again for their men that were taken before; and, as men say, there was not so great a battle upon the sea this forty winters; and forsooth we were well and truly beat, and my Lord hath sent for more ships, and like to fight together again in haste.

No more I write unto you at this time, but that it please you for to recommend me unto my right reverend, and worshipful cousin your husband, and mine uncle Gournay, and to mine aunt his wife, and to all good masters and friends, where it shall please you; and after the writing I have from you, I shall be at you in all haste.

Written on Corpus Christi day in great haste.

By your own humble servant and cousin,

JOHN JERNYNGAN.

XVI. *To my right worshipful husband, John Paston,*
be this delivered in haste.

(Before 1459)

Right worshipful husband, I recommend me to
you, desiring to hear of your welfare, praying you to
weet that Sir Thomas Howes hath purveyed four
dormants for the drawte chamber, and the malthouse
and the brewery, whereof he hath brought three, and
the fourth, that shall be the longest and greatest of
all, he shall have from Heylesdon, which he saith my
master Fastolf shall give me, because my chamber
shall be made therewith. As for the laying of the
said dormants, they shall be laid this next week
because of the malthouse, and as for the remanent,
I trow it shall abide till ye come home because I can
neither be purveyed of posts, nor of boards not yet.

I have taken the measure in the drawte chamber,
there as ye would your coffers and your cowntewery
should be set for the while, and there is no space
beside the bed, though the bed were removed to the
door, to set both your board and your coffers there,
and to have space to go and sit beside; wherefore
I have purveyed that ye shall have the same drawte
chamber that ye had before, thereas ye shall lie to
yourself; and when your gear is removed out of your
little house, the door shall be locked, and your bags
laid in one of the great coffers, so that they shall be
safe, I trust.

Richard Charles and John Dow have fetched
home the child from Rockland Tofts, and it is a pretty
boy; and it is told me that Will is at Blickling with
a poor man of the town; a young woman that was
some time with Burton of this town sent me word
thereof. I pray you send me word if ye will that
anything, that ye will, be done to him ere ye come
home. Richard Charles sendeth you word that Willis
hath been at him here, and offered him to make him
estate in all things according to their indenture, and
if he do the contrary ye shall soon have word.

My mother prayeth you for to remember my sister, and to do your part faithfully ere ye come home, to help to get her a good marriage. It seemeth by my mother's language that she would never be so fain to have been delivered of her as she will now.

It was told here that Knivet, the heir, is for to marry. Both his wife and child be dead, as it was told here; wherefore she would that ye should enquire whether it be so or no, and what his livelihood is, and if ye think that it be for to do, to let him be spoken with thereof.

I pray you that ye be not strange of writing of letters to me betwixt this and that ye come home, if I might, I would have every day one from you. The blessed Trinity have you in his keeping. Written at Norwich on the Tuesday next after the conversion of Saint Paul.

By yours,

MARGARET PASTON.

XVII. *To my right worshipful and right entirely well-beloved cousin, the Viscount Beaumont.*

(Before 1460)

Right worshipful and right entirely well-beloved cousin, I commend me to you with all my heart, desiring to hear and verily to know of your worshipful estate, profit, health and good prosperity, the which I beseech our Lord Jesu ever to maintain and preserve in all worship to his pleasance and to your heart's ease.

Please it you, cousin, to weet, that your well-beloved servant Roger Hunt and a servant of my most dread Lord my husband, one William, yeoman of his ewry, have communed together, and been fully thorough and agreed that the said William shall have his office, if it may please your good Lordship.

Wherefore, cousin, I pray you, as my special trust is in you, that ye will at the instance of my prayer and writing, grant by your letters patent to the said William the foresaid office with such wages and fees as Roger your said servant hath it of you, trusting verily that ye shall find the said William a faithful servant to you, and can and may do you right good service in that office.

And, cousin, in the accomplishment of my desire in this matter, ye may do me a right good pleasure, as God knoweth, whom I beseech for his mercy to have you ever in his blessed governance, and send you good life and long with much good worship.

Written at Framlingham the eighth day of March.

ELIANOR, the Duchess of Norfolk.

XVIII. *To my right worshipful husband, John Paston, be this delivered in haste.*

(1460)

Right worshipful husband, I recommend me to you, praying you to weet that I have received your letter this day that ye sent me by Yelverton's man. As for your signet, I found it upon your board the same day that ye went hence and I send it you by Richard Heberd, bringer hereof. As for your errands that ye wrote to me for, Richard Charles is out about your errands about Gresham, and for his own matters also, and I suppose he cometh not home till it be Tuesday or Wednesday next coming, and as soon as he cometh home he shall go about your errands that ye wrote to me for.

I sent you a letter written on Tuesday last past which as I suppose, Roger Ormsby delivered you. I took it to Alson Partridge; she rode with Clippersby's wife to London.

I pray you if ye have another son that ye will let it be named Harry, in remembrance of your brother Harry; also I pray you that ye would send me dates and cinnamon as hastily as ye may. I have spoken with John Damme of that ye bade me say to him to say to Thomas Note, and he says he was well paid that ye said and thought therein as ye did. **Nerles** I bade him that he should say to the said Thomas therein as it were of himself without your advice or any others; and he said he should so, and that it should be purveyed for this next week at the furthest. The blessed Trinity have you in his keeping. Written at Norwich in haste the Friday next before Candlemas Day.

By your groaning wife,
MARGARET PASTON.

XIX. *To my worshipful husband John Paston, be this delivered in haste.*

(About 1461)

Right worshipful husband, I recommend me to you, desiring heartily to hear of your welfare, praying you that ye will send me word in haste how ye be agreed with Wichingham and Inglos, for that matter that ye spake to me of at your departing, for if I should purvey either wood or hay, it should be bought best cheap betwixt this and Saint Margaret's mass, as it is told me. As for Appleyard, he come not yet to this town since he come from London. I have sent to Sir Bryse to let me have knowledge when he cometh to town, and he hath promised that I shall have knowledge, and when he cometh I shall do your commandment. My mother bade me send you word that Waryn Herman hath daily fished her water all this year, and therefore she prayeth you to do therefore, while ye be at London, as ye think best.

*   *   *   *   *   *   *   *

I pray you that ye will vouchsafe to send me another sugar-loaf, for my old is done, and also that ye will do make a girdle for your daughter for she hath need thereof. The blessed Trinity have you in his keeping.

Written at Norwich in haste, on the Tuesday next before Saint Thomas's day. Paper is deynty.

Yours,
MARGARET PASTON.

XX.   *To my right worshipful husband, John Paston,
       be this letter delivered in haste.*

(Between 1461 and 1465)

Right worshipful husband, I recommend me to
you; please you to weet that I was at Norwich this
week to purvey such things as needeth me against
this winter; and I was at my mother's, and while
I was there, there came in one Wrothe, a kinsman of
Elizabeth Clere's and he sey your daughter and
praised her to my mother, and said that she was a
goodly young woman, and my mother prayed him to
get for her one good marriage if he knew any; and
he said he knew one should be of a 300 marks by
year, the which is Sir John Cley's son, that is
chamberlain with my lady of York, and he is of age
eighteen years old.   If ye think it be for to be spoken
of, my mother thinks that it should be got for less
money now in this world than it should be hereafter,
either that one, or some other good marriage.

Item, I spake with Master John Estgate for
Pykering's matter after your intent of the matter
of the letter that ye sent home, and he said to me he
should write to you how he had done therein, and
so he sent you a letter, the which was sent you
by John Wodehouse's man with other letters.

As for answer (of) other matters, Daubeney telleth
me he wrote to you.   I beseech Almighty God have
you in his keeping.   Written at Caister, the Sunday
next after St. Martin.

By your

MARGARET PASTON.

XXI. *To my cousin, Margaret Paston.*

(Between 1461 and 1465)

Mine own dear sovereign lady, I recommend me
to you, and thank you of the great cheer that ye made
me here to my great cost and charge and labour.   No
more at this time, but that I pray you ye will send me
hither two ells of worsted for doublets, to happe me
this cold winter, and that ye enquire where William
Paston bought his tippet of fine worsted, which is
almost like silk, and if that be much finer than that
ye should buy me after seven or eight shillings, then
buy me a quarter and the nail thereof for collars,
though it be dearer than the other, for I would make
my doublet all worsted for worship of Norfolk, rather
than like Gonner's doublet.

*   *   *   *   *   *   *   *

Item, I shall tell you a tale,
Pampyng and I have picked your male
And taken out pieces five,
For upon trust of Calle's promise we may soon unthrive,
And if Calle bring us hither twenty pound,
Ye shall have your pieces again, good and round ;
Or else, if he will not pay you the value of the pieces, there
To the post do nail his ear,
Or else do him some other wrongs,
For I will no more in his default borrow,
And but if the receiving of my livelihood be better plied
He shall Christ's hour and mine clean tried.
And look ye be merry and take no thought,
For this rhyme is cunningly wrought.
My Lord Percy and all his house
Recommend them to you, dog, cat, and mouse,
And wish ye had been here still,
For they say ye are a good gill.
No more to you at this time,
But God him save that made this rhyme.
Written the ——— of Saint Mathe,
By your true and trusty husband J.P.

XXII. *To my well-beloved son, Sir John Paston,*
       be this delivered in haste.

(Between 1463 and 1466)

I greet you well, and send you God's blessing and
mine, letting you weet that I have received a letter
from you, the which ye delivered to Master Roger at
Lynn, whereby I conceive that ye think ye did not
well that ye departed hence without my knowledge,
wherefore I let you weet I was right evil payd with
you; your father thought, and thinketh yet, that I
was assented to your departing and that hath caused
me to have great heaviness. I hope that he will be
your good father hereafter if ye demean you well, and
do as ye ought to do to him, and I charge you upon
my blessing that in anything touching your father
that should be (to) his worship, profit, or avail, that ye
do your devoir and diligent labour to the furtherance
therein as ye will have my good will, and that shall
cause your father to be better father to you.

It was told me ye sent him a letter to London;
what the intent thereof was I wot not, but though he
take it but lightly, I would ye should not spare to
write to him again as lowly as ye can, beseeching him
to be your good father; and send him such tidings as
be in the country there ye beeth and that ye ware of
your expenses better and ye have been before this
time, and be your own purse-bearer. I trow ye shall
find it most profitable to you.

I would ye should send me word how ye do, and
how ye have shifted for yourself since ye departed
hence, by some trusty man, and that your father
have no knowledge thereof. I durst not let him know
of the last letter that ye wrote to me, because he was
so sore displeased with me at that time.

Item, I would ye should speak with Wykes, and
know his disposition to Jane Walsham, she hath said
since he departed hence but she might have him she
would never be married; her heart is sore set on
him; she told me that he said to her that there was

no woman in the world he loved so well. I would not he should jape her, for she meaneth good faith, and if he will not have her, let me weet in haste, for I shall purvey for her in other wise.

As for your harness and gear that ye left here, it is in Daubeney's keeping, it was never removed since your departing because that he had not the keys. I trow it shall apeyer but if it be taken heed at betimes; your father knoweth not where it is.

I sent your gray horse to Ruston to the farrier, and he saith he shall never be nought to ride neither right good to plough nor to cart; he saith he was splayed and his shoulder rent from the body. I wot not what to do with him.

Your grandam would fain hear some tidings from you; it were well done that ye sent a letter to her how ye do as hastily as ye may, and God have you in his keeping, and make you a good man, and give you grace to do well as I would ye should do.

Written at Caister, the Tuesday next before Saint Edmund the King.

Your mother,

MARGARET PASTON.

I would ye should make much of the parson of Filby, the bearer hereof and make him good cheer, if ye may.

XXIII.   *To my mistress Margaret Paston, be this delivered in haste, at London.*

(1465)

After all humble and most due recommendation, as lowly as I can, I beseech you of your blessing; please it you to weet that I have sent to my father to have an answer of such matters as I have sent to him for in haste, of which matters the greatest of substance is for the manor of Cotton, beseeching you to re-member him of the same matter that I may have an answer in the most hasty wise.

Also I pray you that mine aunt Poynings may be

desired to send me an answer of such matters as she woteth of by him that shall bring me an answer of the matter of Cotton.

Also mother, I beseech you that there may be purveyed some mean that I might have sent me home by the same messenger two pair of hose, one pair black and another pair of russet, which be ready made for me at the hosier's with the crooked back, next to the Black Friar's gate within Ludgate; John Pampyng knoweth him well enough I suppose, and the black hose be paid for, he will send me the russet unpaid for: I beseech you that this gear be not forgotten, for I have not an whole hose for to don; I trow they shall cost both pair 8s.

My brother and my sister Anne, and all the garrison of Heylesdon fare well, blessed be God, and recommend them to you every one.

I pray you visit the Rood of Northdoor and St. Saviour at Bermondsey, among while ye abide in London, and let my sister Margery go with you to pray to them that she may have a good husband ere she come home again; and now I pray you send me some tidings as ye were wont to command me. And the Holy Trinity have you in keeping, and my fair mistress of the Fleet. Written at Norwich, on Holy Rood day.

Your son and lowly servant,

JOHN PASTON, the youngest.

XXIV. *To Mistress Margaret Paston, be this delivered.*

(Before 1466)

Please it you to weet that I send you by Barker, the bearer hereof, three treacle pots of Geane as my apothecary sweareth unto me, and moreover that they were never undone since they came from Geane, whereof ye shall take as many as pleaseth you; nevertheless my brother John sent to me for two, therefore I must beseech you that he may have at the least one; there is one pot that is marked under the bottom two times with these letters—M.P., which pot I have best trust unto, and next him to the wryghe pot, and I mistrust most the pot that hath a krott above on the top, lest that he hath been undone. And also the other two pots be printed with the merchant's mark two times on the covering, and that other pot is but once marked but with one print, notwithstanding I had like oath and promise for one as well as for all.

JOHN PASTON.

XXV   *To master John Paston, or to my mistress his mother, be this letter delivered in haste.*

(1466)

Brother I commend me to you. * * * By Juddy I sent you a letter by Corby within four days before this, and therewith two pots of oil for salads, which oil was as good as might be when I delivered it, and shall be good at the receiving, if it be not mishandled, nor miscarried.

Item, as for tidings, the Earl of Northumberland is home into the North, and my Lord of Gloucester shall after as tomorrow, men say. Also this day Robert of Ratclyff wedded the Lady Dymock at my place in Fleet Street, and my lady and yours, Dame Elizabeth Bouchier, is wedded to the Lord Howard's son and heir. Also Sir Thomas Walgrave is dead, of the sickness that reigneth, on Tuesday, no cheer for you. Also my Lord Archbishop was brought to the Tower on Saturday at night, and on Monday at midnight he was conveyed to a ship, and so into the sea, and as yet I cannot understand whither he is sent, nor what is fallen of him. Men say that he hath offended, but as John Forter saith, some men say nay, but all his meny are disparbled, every man his way, and some that are great clerks, and famous doctors of his, go now again to Cambridge to school.

As for any other tidings I hear none. The Countess of Oxford is still in St. Martin's, I hear no word of her.

The Queen had child, a daughter, but late at Windsor, thereof I trow ye had word. And as for me, I am in like case as I was; and as for my Lord Chamberlain, he is not yet come to town; when he cometh then shall I weet what to do. Sir John of Parr is your friend and mine, and I gave him a fair arming sword within this three days. I heard somewhat by him of a back friend of yours, and you shall know more hereafter.

Written the last day of April.

[Written by Sir John Paston.]

XXVI. *To Mistress Margaret Paston, be this delivered.*

(Probably between 1466 and 1469)

Right worshipful mother, I commend me to you, and beseech you of your blessing and God's; thank you for your tenderness and help both to me, my brother, and servants.

*　　*　　*　　*　　*　　*　　*　　*

The King is come to London, and there came with him, and rode again him, the Duke of Gloucester, the Duke of Suffolk, the Earl of Arundel, the Earl of Northumberland, the Earl of Essex; the Lords Harry and John of Buckingham, the Lord Dacre, the Lord Chamberlain, the Lord Montjoy and many other knights and esquires; the Mayor of London, twenty-two aldermen, in scarlet, and of the craftsmen of the town to the number of two hundred, all in blue.

The King came through Cheap though it were out of his way, because (if he had not) he would not be seen; and he was accompanied in all people with one thousand horse, some harnessed and some not.

My Lord Archbishop came with him from York, and is at the Moor, and my Lord of Oxford rode to have met the King, and he is with my Lord Archbishop at the Moor; and came not to town with the King. Some say, that they were yesterday three miles to the King wards from the Moor; and that the King sent them a messenger, that they should come when that he sent for them. I wot not what to suppose therein.

The King himself hath good language of the Lords of Clarence, of Warwick, and of my Lords of York and of Oxford, saying they be his best friends; but his household men have other language, so what shall hastily fall I cannot say. My Lord of Norfolk shall be here this night. I shall send you more when I know more.

Item, if Ebesham come not home with my Uncle William, that then ye send me the two French books, that he should have written, that he may write them here.

JOHN PASTON, Knight.

XXVII. *To his worshipful brother, John Paston, be this delivered in haste.*

(1467—8)

Right reverend and worshipful brother, after all duties of recommendation, I recommend me to you, desiring to hear of your prosperity and welfare, which I pray God long to continue to his pleasure, and to your heart's desire; letting you weet that I received a letter from you, in the which letter was eight pence with the which I should buy a pair of slippers.

Furthermore certifying you as for the thirteen and four pence which you sent by a gentleman's man, for my board, called Thomas Newton, was delivered to mine hostess, and so to my creancer, Mr. Thomas Stevenson; and he heartily recommended him to you. Also you sent me word in the letter of twelve pounds of figs and eight pounds of raisins: I have them not delivered, but I doubt not I shall have, for Alweder told me of them, and he said that they came after in another barge.

And as for the young gentlewoman, I will certify you how I first fell in acquaintance with her. Her father is dead; there be two sisters of them; the elder is just wedded; at which wedding I was with mine hostess, and also desired by the gentleman himself, called William Swan, whose dwelling is in Eton. So it fortuned that mine hostess reported on me otherwise than I was worthy, so that her mother commanded her to make me good cheer, and so in good faith she did. She is not abiding where she is now, her dwelling is in London, but her mother and she came to a place of hers five miles from Eton, where the wedding was, because it was nigh to the gentleman, which wedded her daughter; and on Monday next coming, that is to say, the first Monday of clean Lent, her mother and she will go to the pardon at Sheen, and so forth to London, and there to abide in a place of hers in Bow Churchyard; and if it please you to enquire of her, her mother's name is Mistress Alborow, the name of the daughter is Margaret Alborow; the age of her is, by all likelihood, eighteen or nineteen years at the farthest. And as for the money and plate, it is ready whensoever she were wedded; but as for the livelihood, I trow not till after her mother's decease, but I cannot tell you for very certain, but you may know by enquiring.

And as for her beauty, judge you that, when you see her, if so be that ye take the labour; and specially behold her hands, for, if it be as it is told me, she is disposed to be thick.

And as for my coming from Eton, I lack nothing but versifying, which I trust to have with a little continuance.

Quare, Quomodo. Non valet hora, valet mora.
Unde dî | o |
Arbore jam videas exemplum. Non die possunt
Omne suppleri, sed tu illa mora.

And these two verses aforesaid be of mine own
making. No more to you at this time, but God have
you in his keeping. Written at Eton the even of
Saint Mathias the Apostle in haste, with the hand of
your brother.

WILLIAM PASTON, Junior.

XXVIII. *To my right reverend and worshipful
mother, Margaret Paston, dwelling at Caister,
be this delivered in haste.*

(1468)

Right reverend and worshipful mother, I recommend me unto you as humbly as I can think, desiring
most heartily to hear of your welfare and heart's ease,
which I pray God send you as hastily as any heart
can think.

Please it you to weet, that at the making of this
bill, my brother and I, and all our fellowship, were in
good hele, blessed be God.

As for the guiding here in this country, it is as
worshipful as all the world can devise, and there were
never Englishmen had so good cheer out of England
that ever I heard of.

As for tidings here, but if it be of the feast, I can
none send you, saving that my Lady Margaret was
married on Sunday last past at a town that is called
The Dame, three miles out of Bruges, at five of the
clock in the morning; and she was brought the same
day to Bruges to her dinner; and there she was
received as worshipfully as all the world could desire,
as with procession with ladies and lords, best beseen
of any people, that ever I saw or heard of.

Many pageants were played in her way in Bruges
to her welcoming, the best that ever I saw; and the
same day my Lord the Bastard, took upon him to
answer twenty-four knights and gentlemen within eight
days at jousts of peace. And when they were answered,
they twenty-four and himself should tourney with other
twenty-five the next day after, which is on Monday next

coming; and they that have jousted with him into this day, have been as richly beseen, and himself also, as cloth of gold, and silk and silver, and goldsmith's work might make them; for of such gear and gold, and pearls, and stones, they of the Duke's court, neither gentlemen nor gentlewomen, they want none; for without that they have it by wishes, by my troth, I heard never of so great plenty as here is.

This day my Lord Scales jousted with a lord of this country, but not with the Bastard, for they made promise at London, that none of them both should never deal with (the) other in arms; but the Bastard was one of the lords that brought the Lord Scales into the field; and of misfortune a horse struck my Lord Bastard on the leg, and hath hurt him so sore, that I can think he shall be of no power to accomplish up his arms; and that is great pity, for by my troth, I trow God made never a more worshipful knight.

And as for the Duke's court, as of lords, ladies, and gentlewomen, knights, esquires and gentlemen, I heard never of none like to it, save King Arthur's court. And by my troth, I have no wit nor remembrance to write to you half the worship that is here, but what lacketh, as it cometh to mind I shall tell you when I come home, which I trust to God shall not be long to fore. We depart out of Bruges homeward on Tuesday next coming, and all folk that came with my Lady of Burgundy out of England except such as shall abide here still with her, which I wot well shall be but few.

We depart the sooner, for the Duke hath word that the French king is purposed to make war upon him hastily, and that he is within four or five days' journey of Bruges and the Duke rideth, on Tuesday next coming, forward to meet with him; God give him good speed and all his, for by my troth they are the goodliest fellowship that ever I came amongst and best can behave them, and most like gentlemen.

Other tidings have we none here, but that the Duke of Somerset and all his bands departed well beseen out of Bruges a day before my Lady the

Duchess came thither, and they say here, that he is (gone) to Queen Margaret that was, and shall no more come here again, nor be holpen by the Duke.

No more, but I beseech you of your blessing as lowly as I can, which I beseech you forget not to give me every day once. And, mother, I beseech you that ye will be good mistress to my little man, and to see that he go to school.

I sent my cousin Daubeney five shillings by Calle's man, for to buy for him such gear as he needeth, and mother, I pray you this bill may recommend me to my sisters both, and to the master, my cousin Daubeney, Sir James, Sir John Stylle, and to pray him to be good master to little Jack and to learn him well, and I pray you that this bill may recommend me to all your folks and to my wellwishers. And I pray God send you your heart's desire.

Written at Bruges the Friday next after Saint Thomas.

Your son, and humble servant,

J. PASTON, the Younger.

XXIX. *To John Paston, the younger, be this delivered in haste.*

(Between 1466 and 1470.)

I greet you well and send you God's blessing and mine, letting you weet that since ye departed my cousin Calthorpe sent me a letter complaining in his writing that forasmuch as he cannot be paid of his tenants as he hath been before this time, he proposeth to lessen his household and to live the straitlier, wherefore he desireth me to purvey for your sister Anne; he saith she waxeth high and it were time to purvey her a marriage. I marvel what causeth him to write so now, either she hath displeased him or else he hath taken her with default; therefore I pray you commune with my cousin Clere at London and weet how he is disposed to her ward, and send me word, for I shall be fain to send for her, and with me she shall but lose her time, and without she will be the better occupied she shall often times move me and put me in great inquietness. Remember what labour I had with your sister, therefore do your part to help her forth, that may be to your worship and mine.

Item, remember the bill that I spake to you of to get of your brother of such money as he hath received of me since your father's decease; see your uncle Maultby if ye may, and send me some tidings as soon as ye may; God keep you. Written the Friday next before Saint Thomas of Canterbury, in haste.

By your mother,

MARGARET PASTON.

XXX. *To my right well-beloved brother John Paston Esq. being at Caister, or to John Daubeney there, be this letter delivered.*

(1468)

Right well-beloved brother, I commend me to you, letting you weet that I have waged, for to help you and Daubeney to keep the place at Caister, four well assured and true men to do all manner of things that they be desired to do in safeguard or inforcing of the said place, and moreover they be proved men, and cunning in war and in feats of arms, and they can well shoot both guns and cross-bows, and amend and string them, and devise bulwarks, or any things that should be a strength to the place, and they will, as need is, keep watch and ward. They be sad and well-advised men, saving one of them, which is bald and called William Peny, which is as good a man as goeth on the earth saving a little. He will, as I understand, be a little copschotyn, but yet he is no brawler, but full of courtesy, much upon James Halman. The other three be named Peryn Sale, John Chapman, Robert Jackson, saving that as yet they have none harness come, but when it cometh it

shall be sent to you, and in the meanwhile I pray you
and Daubeney to purvey them some.

Also a couple of beds they must needs have, which
I pray you by the help of my mother to purvey for
them till that I come home to you. Ye shall find them
gentlemanly comfortable fellows, and that they will
and dare abide by their tackling, and if ye understand
that any assault should be towards, I send you these
men, because that men of the country thereabout you
should be frayed for fear of loss of their goods;
wherefore if there were any such thing towards, I
would ye took of men of the country but few, and
that they were well assured men, for else they might
discourage all the remanent.

*　*　*　*　*　*　*　*

Written on Wednesday next before St Martin.

JOHN PASTON.

*　*　*　*　*　*　*　*

Also, that these men be at the beginning entreated
as courteously as ye can.

Also, I pray you to send me my flower by the next
messenger that cometh.

*　*　*　*　*　*　*　*

Also, as for the Bible that the master hath, I
thought the utmost price had not past five marks, and
so I trow he will give it, weet I pray you.

XXXI. *To my Mother and to my Brother John Paston.*

(1469 or 1474)

Brother, it is so that the King shall come into
Norfolk in haste, and I wot not whether that I may
come with him or not; if I come I must do make a livery
of twenty gowns, which I must pick out by your advice;
and as for the cloth for such persons as be in that
country, if it might be had there at Norwich or not,
I wot not; and what persons I am not remembered.

If my mother be at Caister, as there shall be no doubt, for the keeping of the place while the King is in that country, that I may have the most part at Caister; and whether ye will offer yourself to wait upon my Lord of Norfolk or not, I would ye did that best were to do; I would do my lord pleasure and service, and so I would ye did, if I wist to be sure of his good lordship in time to come. He shall have two hundred in a livery blue and tawny, and blue on the left side, and both dark colours.

I pray you send me word, and your advice by Juddy of what men and what horse I could be purveyed of, if so be that I must needs come, and of your advice in all things by writing, and I shall send you hastily other tidings. Let Sorrell be well kept.

JOHN PASTON, Kt.

XXXII. *To Sir John Paston, knight.*

(1469)

Right worshipful Sir, I recommend me unto you, and as for the certainty of the deliverance of Caister, John Chapman can tell you how that we were enforced thereto, as well as myself. As for John Chapman and his three fellows I have purveyed that they be paid each of them 40 shillings with the money that they had of you and Daubeney; and that is enough for the season that they have done you service; I pray you give them their thank, for by my troth they have as well deserved it as any men that ever bore life; but as for money ye need not to give them without ye will, for they be pleased with their wages.

Wryttill promised me to send you the certainty of the appointment, we were for lack of victuals, gunpowder, men's hearts, lack of surety of rescue, driven thereto to take appointment.

. If ye will that I come to you, send me word and I shall purvey me for to tarry with you a two or three days; by my troth the rewarding of such folks as hath been with me during the siege, hath put me in great danger for the money. God preserve you, and I pray you be of good cheer till I speak with you, and I trust to God to ease your heart in some things.

John Paston.

XXXIII. *To John Paston, Esquire, be this delivered.*

(1469—70)

*   *   *   *   *   *   *   *

Also I pray you speak to Playters that there may be found a mean that the Sheriff or the gatherer of the green-wax may be discharged of certain issues that ran upon Fastolf for Maryot's matter, for the bailiff was at him this week and should have distrained him, but that he promised him that he should within this eight days labour the means that he should be discharged, or else he must content him, etc.,

Also I send you by the bearer hereof, closed in this letter, 5s. of gold and pray you to buy me a sugar loaf, and dates and almonds, and send it me home, and if ye beware any more money, when ye come home I shall pay it you again. The Holy Ghost keep you both and deliver you of your enemies. Written on Saint Agas Day, in haste.

Item, I pray you speak to Master Roger for my syrup, for I had never more need thereof, and send it me as hastily as ye can.

By

Margaret Paston.

XXXIV. *To Sir John Paston, Knight.*

(1469—70)

Right worshipful and my especial true-hearted friend, I commend me unto you, praying you to ordain me three horses' harness as goodly as ye and Genyns can devise, as it were for yourself, and that I may have them in all haste, order. Also Skern saith, ye would ordain two standard staves. This I pray you to remember and my wife shall deliver you silver, and yet she must borrow it. Six or seven pounds I would bestow on a horse harness, and so Skern told me I might have. The Lord Hastings had (one) for the same price, but I would not mine were like his: and I trust to God we shall do right well, who preserve you. Written at Canterbury in haste, the 18th day of July.

OXYNFORD.

XXXV. *To my right worshipful Mother,*
       Margaret Paston, at Mawteby.

(Between 1470 and 1474)

Right Worshipful Mother, after all humble re-commendations, as lowly as I can, I beseech you of your blessing.

Please you to weet that late yester night I came to Norwich, purposing to have been at this day with you at Mawteby, but it is so that I may not hold my purpose, for he that shall pay me my quarter wages for me and my retinue is in Norwich, and waiteth hourly when his money shall come to him. It is one Edmund Bowen of the Exchequer, a special friend of mine, and he adviseth me to tarry till the money be come, lest that I be unpaid, "for who cometh first to the mill, first must grind."

And as I was writing this bill, one of the grooms of my lord's chamber came to me, and told me that my lady will be here in Norwich tomorrow at night towards Walsingham, which shall, I wot well, be another let to me, but I had more need to be otherwise occupied than to await on ladies, for there is as yet, I trow, no spear that shall go over the sea so evil horsed as I am, but it is told me that Richard Calle hath a good horse to sell, and one John Butcher of Oxborough hath another, and if it might please you to give Sym leave to ride into that country at my cost, and in your name, saying that ye will give one of your sons a horse, desiring him that he will give you a pennyworth for a penny, and he shall, and the price be reasonable, hold him pleased with your payment out of my purse, though he know it not ere his horse depart from his hands. Mother, I beseech you, and it may please you to give Sym leave to ride on this message in your name that he may be here with me tomorrow in the morning betimes, for were I once horsed, I trow I were as far forth ready as some of my neighbours.

I heard a little word that ye purposed to be here in Norwich the next week, I pray God it be this week.

Mother, I beseech you that I may have an answer tomorrow at the farthest of this matter and of any other service that it please you to command me, which I will at all seasons (be) ready to accomplish with God's grace, whom I beseech to preserve you and yours.

Written at Norwich, this Wednesday in Easter week.

By your son and servant,

JOHN PASTON.

XXXVI. *To his well-beloved John Paston, Esquire,
at Norwich, or to Mrs Margaret, his Mother.*

(1471)

I commend me to you..........I would fain have the
measure where my father lieth at Bromholm; both
the thickness, and compass of the pillar at his head,
and from that the space to the altar, and the thickness of that altar and imagery of timber work and
what height the arch is to the ground of the aisle, and
how high the ground of the choir is higher than the
ground of the aisle.

Item, I pray you let the measure by packthread be
taken, or else measured by yard, how much is from
the North Gate, where the brigg was at Gresham to
the south wall and in like form from the east side to
the west, also the height of the east wall, and the
height of the south-east tower from the ground, if ye
may easily.   Also what breadth every tower is within
the wall and which tower is more than other within.
Also how many foot or what breadth each tower
taketh within each corner of the quadrate overthwart
the doors, and how many tailor's yards is from the
mote side where the brigg was to the highway, or to
the hedge all along the entry, and what breadth the
entry is between the dykes.

I pray you, if ye have a leisure in any wise, see this
done yourself if ye may, or else if Pampyng do it, or
who that ye think can do it, I would spend twenty
pence or as ye seem, to have the certain of every
thing herein.

And as for my father's tomb, I charge you see it
yourself, and when I speak with you, I will tell you
the causes why that I desire this to be done.

As for tidings, the King and the Queen and much
other people are ridden and gone to Canterbury, never
so much people seen in pilgrimage heretofore at once,
as men say.

Also it is said that the Earl of Pembroke is taken
into Brittany, and men say that the King shall have

delivery of him hastily, and some say that the King of France will see him safe and shall set him at liberty again.

Item, Thomas Fauconbridge his head was yesterday set upon London Bridge looking into Kent ward, and men say that his brother was sore hurt and escaped to sanctuary to Beverley. Sir Thomas Fulforth escaped out of Westminster with a hundred spears as men say, and is into Devonshire and there he hath stricken off Sir John Crokker's head, and killed another knight of the Courtenays as men say. I would ye had your very pardon at once, wherefore I pray you fail not to be at London within four days after Saint Faith's; ye shall do good in many things, and I pray you send me word hereof by the next messenger, and if it come to Mrs Elizabeth Higgens, at the Black Swan, she shall convey it to me, for I will not fail to be there at London again within this six days.

Mrs Elizabeth hath a son, and was delivered within two days after Saint Bartholomew, and her daughter A. H. was, the next day after, delivered of another son, as she saith eleven weeks ere her time. It was christened John, and is dead, God save all. No more till I speak with you.

Written at London on Michaelmas Even.

JOHN PASTON, Knight.

XXXVII. *To my right worshipful brother, Sir John Paston, Knight.*

(1472, or perhaps 1470)

Right worshipful sir, I recommend me to you.........
Item, Master John Smythe telleth me, that Sir T. Lyney's goods are not able to pay a quarter of his debts that be asked him, wherefore such money as is beleft, must be divided to every man a part after the quantity, which division is not yet made, but when it

is made he hath promised me that your part shall be worth three the best, etc.

Item, as for one of Berney's horse, whoso hath least need to him, he shall cost him twenty marks not a penny less.

Ye sent me word of the marriage of my Lady Jane; one marriage for another one, Norse and Bedford were asked in the church on Sunday last past.

As for my sister Anne, my Mother will not remove from W. Yelverton for Bedyngfield, for she hath communed farther in that matter, since ye were in this country, as it appeareth in her letter, that she sendeth you by Thyrston.

*   *   *   *   *   *   *   *

John Osbern adviseth you to take breath for the wood sale at Sporle, for he hath cast it, that it is worth as good as nine score pounds. Beware of Montayn, for he may not pay you so much money with his ease.

I pray you recommend me to Sir John Parr with all my service, and tell him by my troth, I longed never sorer to see my lady than I do to see his mastership; and I pray God that he arise never a morning from my lady his wife, without it be against her will, till such time as he bring her to Our Lady of Walsingham.

Also I pray you to recommend me in my most humble wise unto the good Lordship of the most courteous, gentlest, wisest, kindest, most companionable, freest, largest, and most bounteous knight, my Lord the Earl of Arran, which hath married the King's sister of Scotland. Hereto he is one the lightest, delyverst, best spoken, fairest archer; devoutest, most perfect and truest to his lady of all the knights that ever I was acquainted with. So would God my lady liked me as well as I do his person and most knightly conditions, with whom I pray you to be acquainted, as (to) you seemeth best; he is lodged at the George in Lombard Street. He hath a book of my sister Anne's of the siege of Thebes; when he hath done with it, he promised to deliver it you. I pray you let Portland bring the book home with him. Portland is lodged at the George in Lombard Street also.

And this I promise you, ye shall not be so long again without a bill from me, as ye have been, though I should write how oft the wind changeth, for I see by your writing ye can be wrath, and ye will, for little.

Written the fifth day of June.

JOHN PASTON.

XXXVIII. *To John Paston, Esquire, at Norwich, be this delivered.*

(1473)

Worshipful and well-beloved brother, I commend me to you, letting you weet, that the world seemeth queasy here, for the most part that be about the King have sent hither for their harness, and it (is) said for certain, that the Duke of Clarence maketh him big in that he can, shewing as he would but deal with the Duke of Gloucester, but the King intendeth, in eschewing all inconvenience, to be as big as they both, and to be a stiffler atween them, and some men think, that under this there should be some other thing intended, and some treason conspired, so what shall fall, can I not say.

Item, it is said that yesterday two passagers of Dover were taken, I fear that if Juddy had no hasty passage, so that if he passed not on Sunday or Monday, that he is taken, and some gear of mine, that I would not for £20. I hope and purpose to go to Calais-ward on Sunday or Monday or nigh by, for I came not accompanied to do any service here; wherefore it were better for me to be out of sight.

*   *   *   *   *   *   *   *

Item, Spring, that waited on my father when he

was in gaol house, whom my father, at his dying beset
40s. he cryeth ever on me for it, and in way of alms,
and he would be eased, though it were but twenty
shillings, or ten shillings, wherefore he hath written to
my mother, and must have an answer again; I would
that my mother send him, as though she lend him
somewhat, and he will be pleased, and else he can say
as shrewdly as any man in England.

Item, the King hath sent for his great seal; some
say we shall have a new Chancellor, but some think
that the King doth as he did at the last fields, he will
have the seal with him, but this day Doctor Morton,
Master of the Rolls, rideth to the King, and beareth
the seals with him.

Item, I had never more need of money than now,
wherefore Fastolf's five marks and the money of
Master John Smith would make me whole.

Written on St Leonard's day, in the thirteenth
year of the reign of Edward IV.

Item, send me my vestment, according to the
letter I sent you by Symond Dam, in all haste.

JOHN PASTON, Knight.

XXXIX. *To John Paston, Esquire, be this delivered.*

(1473)

Right worshipful brother, I recommend me to you,
letting you weet that this day I was in very purpose
to Calais ward, all ready to have gone to the barge,
save I tarried for a young man that I thought to have
had with me thither, one that was with Rows, which
is in the country; and because I could not get him,
and that I have no more here with me but Pampyng,
Edward, and Jack, therefore Pampyng remembered
me that at Calais he told me, that he purposed to be
with the Duchess of Norfolk, my lady and yours.
And Edward is sick, and seemeth not abiding; he

would see what shall fall of this world; and so I am as he that saith "Come hither, John, my man". And as hap was yesterday, Juddy went before to Calais ward, wherefore I am now ill purveyed; which for aught that I know yet, is like to keep me here this Whitsuntide. Wherefore if ye know any likely men, and fair conditioned, and good archers, send them to me, though it be four, and I will have them, and they shall have four marks by the year, and my livery.

He may come to me hither to the Goat, or yet to Calais with a rial if he be wise, which if need be, I would that Barker took him to come up with, if it be such one as ye trust.

Item, I suppose both Pytt and Kothye Plattyng shall go from me in haste; I will never cherish knaves so as I have done, for their sakes.

Item, I pray you send me a new vestment of white damask for a deacon, which is amongst mine other gear at Norwich, for he shall thereto as ye wot of; I will make an arming doublet of it, though I should another time give a long gown of velvet for another vestment, and send it in all haste to Hoxon to send me.

I hoped to have been very merry at Calais this Whitsuntide and am well apparelled and appointed, save that these folks fail me so, and I have matter there to make of right excellent. Some man would have hasted him to Calais, though he had had no better errand, and some men think it wisdom and profit to be there now well out of the way.

*   *   *   *   *   *   *   *

No more but God keep you. Written at London the 3rd day of June, in the thirteenth year of Edward IV.

JOHN PASTON, Knight.

XL. *To Edmund Paston, Esquire, at
Calais, be this delivered.*

(1473)

Brother Edmund, I greet you well, letting you
weet that about this day se'night I sent you a letter
by Nicholas Bardesley, a soldier, which is wont to be
at (the) border perauntys; and also a hosecloth of
black for you; I wend that ye should have had it
within two days, but I am afraid that he deceived me.

Item, I let you weet that Plattyng is coming
hither, and he saith that ye gave him leave to fetch
his gear and Pytt's; and that is his errand hither and
none other, nor he thought never to go from me, nor
will he not go from me, as he saith; wherefore I pray
you send me word of his conditions, and why ye think
that he should never do me worship.

He saith also, that he and Pytt were at the taking
of the Esterlings, and that he was in the "Packer"
and Pytt in the "Christopher"; I pray you send me
word how both he and Pytt quit them, by the report
of some indifferent true man that was there; if they
quit them well, I would love them the better;
wherefore the next day after the sight of this letter,
I pray you write again, and send it by the next passage.

Item, I send you a little pretty box herewith,
which I would that Juddy should deliver to the
woman that he weeteth of, and pray her to take it to
the man that she weeteth of; that is to say, as much
as ye know all well enough, but ye may not make you
wise in no wise.

Item, I pray you send me word as ye were wont to
do of her welfare, and whether I were out and other
in or not; and whether she shall forsake Calais as
soon as ye sent me word of, or not.

By God I would be with you as fain as yourself,
and shall be in haste, with God's grace.

Item, as for my brother John, I hope within this
month to see him in Calais, for by likelihood tomorrow,
or else the next day, he taketh ship at Yarmouth, and

goeth to Saint James-ward, and he hath written to
me that he will come homeward by Calais.

Item, I suppose that James Songer shall come
with me to Calais, the rather for your sake.

Item, Mistress Elizabeth fareth well, but as yet
Songer knoweth not so perfectly all that ye would
weet, that he will not write to you of these two days,
till he know more; but if she had been bold, and
durst have abided still at her gate, and spoken with
me, so God help me, she had had this same (box) that
I send now, where ye wot of, which ye shall see worn
hereafter; it is a pretty ribbon with pretty aglets and
goodly.

Make you not wise to Juddy neither not that ye
would weet anything, for I may say to you, at his
coming over he brought goodly gear reasonably.

Item, as for my bill that is gilt, I would it were
taken heed to; there is one in the town, that can
glaze well enough as I heard say; also there is one
cometh every market day from St Omers to Calais,
and he bringeth daggers and fetcheth also, he may
have it with him, and bring it again the next market
day for 12*d.* or 16*d.* at the most; and else let it be
well oiled and kept till I come.

No more. Written at London the 5th day of
July, in the thirteenth year of Edward IV.

JOHN PASTON, Knight.

XLI. *To John Paston, Esquire.*

(1474)

Brother, I recommend me to you letting you weet,
that I have, like as I promised you, I have done my
devoir to know my Lady Walgrave's stomach, which,
as God help me, and to be plain to you, I find in her
no matter nor cause, that I might take comfort of.

She will in no wise receive nor keep your ring
with her, and yet I told her that she should not be
anything bound thereby; but that I knew by your

heart of old that I wist well ye would be glad to forbear the levest thing that ye had in the world, which might be daily in her presence, that should cause her once on a day to remember you; but it would not be. She would not thereby, as she said, put you nor keep you in any comfort thereby. And moreover, she prayed me, that I should never take labour more herein, for she would hold herself to such answer as she had given you tofore; wherewith she thought both ye and I would have held us content, had (it) not been (for) the words of her sister Genevieve. When I understood all this, and that over night she bade her that went between her and me bid me bring with me her muskball which etc., then I after all this, asked if she were displeased with me for it, and she said, nay.

Then I told her, that I had not sent it you, for sin of my soul; and so I told her all, how I had written to you why that I would not send it you, because I wist well ye should have sleeped the worse; but now I told her, as God help me, that I would send it you, and give you mine advice not to hope over much on her, which is over hard an hearted lady for a young man to trust unto; which I thought that for all my words, ye could not nor would not do for all mine advice.

Yet againwards she is not displeased, nor forbid me not but that ye should have the keeping of her muskball; wherefore do ye with it as ye like. I would it had done well; by God I spake for you so, that in faith I trow I could not say so well again. Wherefore I send you herewith your ring and the unhappy muskball. Also make ye matter of it hereafter as ye can, I am not happy to woo neither for myself nor none other. I told her all the process of the Lord Howard and of your grounds as I could; all helps not.

*   *   *   *   *   *   *   *

I hear no word of my vessel nor of my books; I marvel. No more. Written at London the 11th day of December in the fourteenth year of Edward IV.

JOHN PASTON, Knight.

XLII.   *[This letter has no direction, but it is
        written either to John Paston, Esquire, or
        Margaret Paston.]*

(1475)

Like it you to weet, that not in the most happy
season for me, it is so fortuned, that whereas my
Lord of Norfolk, yesterday being in good health, this
night died about midnight, wherefore it is for all that
loved him to do and help now that, that may be to
his honour, and weal to his soul. And it is so, that
this country is not well purveyed of cloth of gold for
the covering for his body and herse; wherefore every
man helping to his power, I put the Council of my
lord in comfort, that I hoped to get one for that day,
if it were so that it be not broken, or put to other use.

Wherefore please it you to send me word if it be
so, that ye have, or can come by, the cloth of tissue,
that I bought for our father's tomb, and I undertake
it shall be saved again for you unhurt at my peril; I
deem hereby to get great thanks, and great assistance
in time to come; and that either Sym or Mother
Brown may deliver it me tomorrow by seven of the
clock.

Item, as for other means, I have sent my servant
Richard Toring to London, which I hope shall bring
me good tidings again; and within four days I hope to
see you.

Written on Wednesday the 17th day of January,
in the fifteenth year of Edward IV.

JOHN PASTON, Knight.

XLIII. *To John Paston Esquire, at Norwich, be this delivered.*

(1475)

*   *   *   *   *   *   *   *

Item, I wend to have found a gown of mine here, but it came home the same day that I came out, brought by Harry Barker, loader. I would in all haste possible have that same gown of puke furred with white lamb.

Item, I would have my long russet gown of the French russet in all haste, for I have no gown to go in here.

Item, I pray you recommend me to my mother, and let us all pray God send my lady of Norfolk a son, for upon that resteth much matter; for if the king's son marry my lord's daughter, the king would that his son should have a fair place in Norfolk, though he should give me two times the value in other land as I am done to weet. I pray you send me word of my lady's speed as soon as ye can.

Item, as for Bowen I shall feel him, and should have done though ye had not sent.

Item, there is offered me a good marriage for my sister Anne, Skipwith's son and heir of Lincolnshire, a man (of) 500 or 600 marks by the year.

No more. Written at London, the 27th day of January, in the fifteenth year of Edward IV.

Item, my lady of Exeter is dead, and it was said, that the old Duchess of Norfolk and the Countess of Oxford were dead, but it is not so yet.

Item, I shall remember Calais both for horse and all, etc.

[JOHN PASTON, Knight.]

XLIV.   *Unto my right well-beloved Valentine, John*
Paston, Esquire, be this bill delivered, etc.

(1476—7)

Right reverend and worshipful and my right
well-beloved Valentine, I recommend me unto you,
full heartily desiring to hear of your welfare, which I
beseech Almighty God long for to preserve unto His
pleasure and your heart's desire.   And if it please
you to hear of my welfare, I am not in good heele of
body, nor of heart, nor shall be till I hear from you:

> For there wottys no creature what pain that I endure,
> And for to be dead, I dare it not discur'.

And my lady my mother hath laboured the matter
to my father full diligently, but she can no more get
than ye know of, for the which God knoweth I am full
sorry.   But if that ye love me, as I trust verily that
ye do, ye will not leave me therefore; for if that ye
had not half the livelihood that ye have, for to do the
greatest labour that any woman alive might, I would
not forsake you.

> And if ye command me to keep me true wherever I go,
> I wis I will de all my might you to love, and never no mo(re).
> And if my friends say, that I do amiss,
> They shall not me let so for to do,
> Mine heart me bids ever more to love you
> Truly over all earthly thing,
> And if they be never so wrath
> I trust it shall be better in time coming.

No more to you at this time, but the Holy Trinity
have you in keeping.   And I beseech you that this
bill be not seen of none earthly creature save only
yourself, etc.

And this letter was endited at Topcroft, with full
heavy heart, etc.

By your own

MARGERY BREWS.

XLV. *To my right well-beloved cousin John Paston, Esquire, be this letter delivered, etc.*

(1476—7)

Right worshipful and well-beloved Valentine, in my most humble wise, I recommend me unto you, etc. And heartily I thank you for the letter, which that ye send me by John Beckerton, whereby I understand and know that ye be purposed to come to Topcroft in short time, and without any errand or matter, but only to have a conclusion of the matter betwixt my father and you; I would be most glad of any creature alive so that the matter might grow to effect. And thereas ye say, and ye come and find the matter no more towards you than ye did aforetime, ye would no more put my father and my lady my mother to no cost nor business, for that cause a good while after, which causeth my heart to be full heavy; and if that ye come, and the matter take to none effect, then should I be much more sorry, and full of heaviness.

And as for myself I have done and understand in the matter that I can or may as God knoweth; and I let you plainly understand, that my father will no more money part withal in that behalf, but a hundred pounds and fifty marks, which is right far from the accomplishment of your desire.

Wherefore if that ye could be content with that good, and my poor person, I would be the merriest maiden on ground; and if ye think not yourself so satisfied, or that ye might have much more good, as I have understood by you afore; good, true and loving Valentine, that ye take no such labour upon you, as to come more for that matter, but let (what) is, pass, and never more to be spoken of, as I may be your true lover and beadwoman during my life.

No more unto you at this time, but Almighty Jesu preserve you both body and soul, etc.

By your Valentine,

MARGERY BREWS.

4—2

XLVI. *Unto my right worshipful master, John Paston, Esquire, be this bill delivered, etc.*

(1476—7)

Right worshipful Sir, I recommend me unto you; letting you know, as for the young gentlewoman, she oweth you her good heart and love, as I know by the communication that I have had with her for the same.

And, Sir, ye know what my master and my lady have proffered with her—200 marks—and I daresay that her chamber and arayment shall be worth 100 marks. And I heard my lady say that and the case required, both ye and she should have your board with my lady three years after.

And I understand by my lady that she would that ye should labour the matter to my master, for it should be better. And I heard my lady say,

> "That it was a feeble oak
> That was cut down at the first stroke."

And ye be beholden unto my lady for her good word, for she has never praised you too much. Sir, like as I promised you, I am your man, and my good will ye shall have in word and deed, etc.

And Jesu have you in His merciful keeping, etc.

By your man

THOMAS KELA.

XLVII. *To Master Sir John Paston, be this letter delivered in Calais.*

(1476)

Honour and joy be to you my right good master, and most assured brother: letting you know that all your well-willers and servants in these parts, that I know, fare well and better would if they might hear of your well being, and forthwith some of your French and Burgundy tidings; for we in these parts be in great dread lest the French King with some assaults should in any wise disturb you of your soft, sote and sure sleeps, but as yet we nothing can hear that he so disposeth him.

    *   *   *   *   *   *   *   *

Sir, furthermore, I beseech you as ye will do anything for me, that ye see one day for my sake, and for your own pleasure, all the good horse in Calais, and if there be amongst them any prized horse of deeds, that is to sell, in especial that he be well trotting of his own courage without force of spurs, and also a steering horse, if he be, he is the better. I pray you send me word of his colour, deeds and courage, and also of his price, feigning as ye would buy him yourself, and also I would have him somewhat large, not with the largest, but no small horse, as (no?) more than a double horse; praying you above all things to have this in remembrance and that hastily as may be, for there is late promised me help to such an intent, and I wote not how long it shall endure; and therefore I beseech you send me word by time.

I trow the Frenchmen have taken up all the good horse in Picardy, and also they be wont to be heavy horse in labour, and that I love not; but a heavy horse of flesh and light of courage I love well, for I love no horse that will always be lean and slender like greyhounds. God keep you.

Your
JOHN PYMPE.

I pray you to recommend me to my cousin, Sir John Scot and all his, in especial Mrs Bedingfeld.

XLVIII. *Unto the right Worshipful Sir John Paston, Knight.*

(1477)

Master Paston, after all due recommendation, and hearty desire to hear of your good hele, please it you to weet, I have spoken with Sir John of Middylton, as well as I could and it had been for myself, for his hobby (horse) that ye desired, and told him he might well forbear him now, inasmuch as Mrs Jane was dead, and that it is a great cost for him to keep more horse than he needeth, and he answered me that he would sell him with good will, but there should no man buy him under £10 Flemish; and I offered him in your name 10 marks, for he would not hear of no other ambling horse that ye might give him therefore.

And also my lord desired to have bought him for the Lord Schauntrell that is chief captain of St Omers; and he would (for) no less let my lord have him than £10, and so my lord bought another and gave him the said lord, for he thought this too dear, nevertheless he will not sell him to no man under that money that he set him on, and so ye may buy your pleasure in him and ye list, for otherwise he will not do for you as I conceive.

*   *   *   *   *   *   *   *

And as I understand, the emperor's son is married at Ghent as this day, and there came with him but 400 horse, and I can hear of no more that be coming in certain, and in money he bringeth with him an hundred thousand ducats, which is but a small thing in regard for that he hath to do; wherefore I fear me sore that Flanders will be lost; and if St Omers be won, all is gone in my conceit, nevertheless they say there should come great power after the emperor's son, but I believe it not because they have been so long of coming.

And I pray you to recommend me to Sir Terry Robsart, and that it please you to let him know of your tidings, and our Lord have you in his keeping.

At Calais, the Sunday next after the Assumption.

Your

EDMUND BEDYNGFELD.

XLIX. *To my right worshipful mother, Margaret Paston, be this delivered.*

(1478)

Please it you to weet, that whereas I intended to have been at home this Midsummer, and purposed with your good help to have begun upon my father's tomb, so that it might have been ended this summer; it is so, that for such causes as are now begun between my Lord of Suffolk and me, for the Manors of Heylesdon, Drayton, etc. for which matters I must needs be here this next term; therefore I deem it would be after Midsummer, ere than I can see you.

Please it you also to weet that I communed with Master Pykenham to weet if he would buy the cloth of gold for so much as he desired once to have bought it, and he offered me once 20 marks therefor, nevertheless it cost me £24; yet now, when that I spake to him thereof, he refused to buy it, and said that he had now so many charges that he may not. But it is so that the King doth make certain copes and vestments of like cloth, which he intendeth to give to the College of Fotheringay, where my Lord his father is now buried, and he buyeth at a great price.

I communed with the vestment maker for to help me forth with 12 yards, and he hath granted to do, as Wheatley can tell you; wherefore, if it please you that it be bestowed for to make a tomb for my father at Bromholm, if ye like to send it hither, if it be sold I undertake ere Michaelmas that there shall be a tomb, and somewhat else over my father's grave, on whose soul God have mercy, that there shall none be like it in Norfolk; and as ye shall be glad hereafter to see it; and God send me leisure that I may come home, and if I do not, yet the money shall be put to none other use, but kept by some other that ye trust, till that it may be bestowed according as is above written, and else I give you cause never to trust me while ye and I live. When I was last with you, ye granted that the said cloth of gold should be bewared about this work, that is above written, which if ye will perform, I undertake that there shall be such a tomb as ye shall be pleased with, though it cost me twenty marks of mine own purse beside, if I once set upon it.

No more, but I beseech God have you in his keeping.

Written at London the Wednesday in Whitsun week, in the eighteenth year of Edward IV.

Please it you to send me word by Wheatley of your pleasure herein.

By your son,

JOHN PASTON, Knight.

L. *To the right worshipful Sir John Paston, Knight.*

(1478)

I greet you well and send you God's blessing and mine, letting you weet that I have sent you by Wheatley the cloth of gold, charging you that it be not sold to none other use than to the performing of your father's tomb as ye sent me word in writing; if ye sell it to any other use, by my troth, I shall never trust you while I live.

Remember that it cost me twenty marks, the pledging out of it, and if I were not glad to see that made, I would not depart from it. Remember what charge I have had with you of late, which will not be for my ease this two years; when ye may, better, I trust ye will remember it.

My cousin Clere doth as much cost at Bromholm as will draw an hundred pounds upon the desks in the choir, and in other places, and Heydon in likewise, and if there should nothing be done for your father it would be too great a shame for us all, and in chief to see him lie as he doth.

Also as I understand it, my cousin Robert Clere thinketh great unkindness in dealing with him of

Peacock, for certain pasture that ye granted him to have and Peacock hath let it to others such as he list to let it to, notwithstanding my cousin hath laid the pasture with his cattle, and Peacock has distrained them.

I think this dealing is not as it should be. I would that each of you would do for other and live as kinsmen and friends; for such servants may make trouble betwixt you, which were against courtesy so nigh neighbours as ye be. He is a man of substance and worship and so will be taken in this shire; and I were loath that ye should lose the goodwill of such as may do for you.

Item, whereas ye have begun your claim in Heylesdon and Drayton I pray God send you good speed, and furtherance in it. Ye have as good a season as ye would wish, considering that your adversary stands not in best favour with the King.

Also ye have the voice in this country, that ye may do as much with the King as any knight that is belonging to the court. If it be so, I pray God continue it, and also that ye should marry right nigh of the Queen's blood; what she is we are not as certain, but if it be so that your land should come again by the reason of your marriage and to be set in rest, at the reverence of God forsake it not, if ye can find in your heart to love her, so that she be such one as ye can think to have issue by, or else by my troth, I had rather that ye never married in your life.

Also, if your matter take not now to good effect, ye and all your friends may repent them that ye began your claim, without that ye have taken such a sure way as may be to your intent for many inconveniences that may fall thereof. God send you good speed in all your matters.

Written at Mauteby, the day after St. Austin, in May, the eighteenth year of King Edward IV.

By your Mother.

LI. *To the right worshipful Mistress Margaret Paston, be this delivered.*

(1479)

Pleaseth it you to weet that I have been here at London a fortnight, whereof the first four days I was in such fear of the sickness, and also found my chamber and stuff not so clean as I deemed, which troubled me sore ; and as I told you at my departing, I was not well monied, for I had not past ten marks whereof I departed forty shillings to be delivered of my old bedfellow ; and then I rode beyond Dunstable and there spake with one of my chief witnesses which promised me to take labour, and to get me writings touching this matter between me and the Duke of Suffolk, and I rewarded him twenty shillings and then as I informed you, I paid five marks incontinent upon my coming here to repledge out my gown of velvet and other gear.   And then I hoped to have borrowed some of Townshend, and he hath foodyd not forth ever since, and in effect I could have at the most and at the soonest yesterday twenty shillings, wherefore I beseech you to purvey me an hundred shillings, and also to write to Peacock, that he purvey me as much, an hundred shillings, which I suppose he hath gathered at Paston and other places by this time ; for without I have this ten pounds, as God help me, I fear I shall do but little good in no matter, nor yet I wote not how to come home but if I have it.

This gear has troubled me so, that it hath made me more than half sick, as God help me.

*   *   *   *   *   *   *   *

Written in haste with short advisement on the Friday next St. Simon and Jude in the nineteenth year of Edward IV.

Let my brother John see this bill, for he knoweth more of the matter.

JOHN PASTON, Knight.

LII. *To my right worshipful husband,*
        John Paston.

(1484)

Right worshipful husband, I recommend me unto
you.   Please it you to weet, that I sent your eldest
son to my Lady Morley to have knowledge what
sports were used in her house in Christmas next
following after the decease of my lord, her husband.
And she said that there were none disguisings, nor
harpings, nor luting, nor singing nor none loud
disports, but playing at the tables, and chess and
cards. Such disports she gave her folks leave to play
and none other.

Your son did right well as ye shall hear after this.
I sent your younger son to the Lady Stapleton, and
she said according to my Lady Morley's saying in
that, and as she had seen used in places of worship
thereas she hath been.

I pray you that ye will assure to you some man at
Caister, to keep your buttery, for the man that ye
left with me will not take upon him to breve daily as
ye commanded.   He saith he hath not used to give a
reckoning neither of bread nor ale, till at the week's
end, and he saith he wot well that he should not
condeneth, and therefore I suppose he shall not abide,
and I trow ye shall be fain to purvey another man for
Symond, for ye are never the nearer a wise man for
him.

I am sorry that ye shall not at home be for
Christmas.

I pray you that ye will come as soon as ye may.
I shall think myself half a widow, because ye shall
not be at home, etc. God have you in his keeping.
Written on Christmas Even.

By your servant and beadwoman

MARGERY PASTON.

LIII. *To my well-beloved friend John Paston,*
be this bill delivered in haste.

(1485)

Well-beloved friend, I commend me to you; letting
you to understand that the king's enemies be a-land,
and that the king would have set forth as upon Monday, but only for our Lady-day; but for certain he
goeth forward as upon Tuesday, for a servant of mine
brought to me the certainty.

Wherefore I pray you that ye meet with me at
Bury, for, by the grace of God, I purpose to lie at
Bury as upon Tuesday night; and that ye bring with
you such company of tall men as ye may goodly make
at my cost and charge, besides that which ye have
promised the king; and I pray you, ordain them
jackets of my livery, and I shall content you at your
meeting with me.

Your lover,

J. NORFOLK.

LIV. *Unto John Paston, in haste.*

(Date uncertain)

Master Paston, I pray that it may please you to
leave your lodging for three or four days, till I may be
purveyed of another, and I shall do as much to your
pleasure; for God's sake, say me not nay, and I pray
you recommend me to my Lord Chamberlain.

Your friend,

ELIZABETH.

LV. *To Mistress Anne.*

(Date uncertain)

Since it is so that I may not as oft as I would be there, as I might do my message myself, mine own fair Mistress Anne, I pray you to accept this bill for my messenger, to recommend me to you in my most faithful wise, as he that fainest of all other desireth to know of your welfare, which I pray God increase to your most pleasure.

And, mistress, though so be that I as yet have given you but easy cause to remember me for lack of acquitation, yet I beseech you let me not be forgotten, when ye reckon up all your servants, to be set in the number with other.

And I pray you, Mistress Anne, for that service that I owe you, that in as short time as ye goodly may that I might be ascertained of your intent, and of your best friends, in such matters as I have broken to you of; which both your and mine right trusty friends John Lee, or else my mistress his wife, promised before you and me at our first and last being together, that as soon as they or either of them knew your intent, and your friends, that they should send me word, and if they so do I trust soon after to see you.

And now farewell, mine own fair lady, and God give you good rest, for in faith I trow ye be in bed.

Written in my way homeward, on Mary Magdalen's day at midnight.

Your own,

JOHN PASTON.

Mistress Anne, I am proud that ye can read English, wherefore I pray you acquaint you with this my lewd hand, for my purpose is that ye shall be more acquainted with it, or else it shall be against my will; but yet and when ye have read this bill, I pray you burn it, or keep it secret to yourself, as my faithful trust is in you.

LVI. *Inventory of English books of John Paston in the reign of Edward IV.*

1. A book had of my hostess at the George...of the Death of Arthur, beginning at Cassibelan.
   Guy Earl of Warwick.
   King Richard Coeur de Lyon.
   A Chronicle to Edward the III.   Price...
2. Item, a book of Troilus, which William Br.......
   hath had near ten years, and lent it to Dame...
   Wyngfeld, and there I saw it...worth...
3. Item, a black book, with the legend of Lad......sans Mercy.
   The Parliament of Birds.
   The Temple of Glass.
   Palatyse and Scitacus.
   The Meditations of...
   The Green Knight...worth...
4. Item, a book in print of the Play of the...
5. Item, a book lent Midelton, and therein is
   Belle Dame sans Mercy.
   The Parliament of Birds.
   Ballad of Guy and Colbrond,
       ...of the Goose, the...
   The Disputation between Hope and Despair.
   ......Merchants.
   The Life of Saint Chrystopher.
6. A red book that Percival Robsart gave me; of the Meeds of the Mass.
   The Lamentation of Child Ipotis.
   A Prayer to the Vernicle, called the Abbey of the Holy Ghost.
7. Item, in quires, Tully de Senectute in whereof there is no more clear writing.
8. Item, in quires, Tully or Cypio de Amicitia, left with William Worcester...worth...
9. Item, in quires, a book of the Policy of In....
10. Item, in quires, a book de Sapientia, wherein the second person is likened to Sapience.

11. Item, a book de Othea, text and gloss, worth in quires...

    Memorandum; mine old book of Blazonings of Arms.

    Item, the new book portrayed and blazoned.

    Item, a copy of Blazonings of Arms, and the... names to be found by Letter.

    Item, a book with Arms portrayed in paper.

    Memorandum; my book of Knighthood; and the manner of making of Knights; of Justs, of Tournaments; fighting in Lists; paces holden by Soldiers; and Challenges; Statutes of War; and de Regimine Principum...worth...

    Item, a book of new Statutes from Edward the IV.

NOTES

LETTER I. **p. 1. William Paston.** Sir W. Paston, knight and judge of the Common Pleas, was born in 1378 and died in 1444.

p. 1. Gentlewoman, Margaret, daughter of John Mauteby of Mauteby in Norfolk, who married John Paston, soon after the writing of this letter.

p. 1. John Paston, son of Sir William and Agnes Paston, was born about 1420, and died in 1466.

p. 1. Pipes of gold, gold thread on pipes or rolls, for needle-work or embroidery.

p. 1. Stews or ponds to keep fish alive for present use.

p. 1. Paston in Norfolk, in the hundred of Tunstead.

p. 1. "Deus qui errantibus," the words beginning the collect on the third Sunday after Easter.

p. 1. Agnes Paston, daughter of Sir Edmond Barry or Berry, of Harlingbury Hall, in Hertfordshire, and wife of Sir William Paston. She died in 1479, and was buried by her husband, in Our Lady's Chapel at the east end of Norwich Cathedral.

LETTER II. **p. 2. behested,** vowed.

p. 2. Another image, this offering of an image of wax, of the weight of the person for whose good it was promised, is an interesting fact.

p. 2. Our Lady of Walsingham. The image of Our Lady of Walsingham, in Norfolk, was in these days, and had been for ages, resorted to by all ranks of people, and was held in very high venera-tion for the various miracles ascribed to her. This famous image was brought to Chelsea in 1538 and burnt there.

p. 2. Four nobles, £1. 6s. 8d.

p. 2. St Leonard's. The Church of the Priory of St Leonard at Norwich was famous at this time as a resort of pilgrims to the images of the Virgin, the Holy Cross, and St Anthony. It afterwards became much more famous through the visitation of pilgrims from far and near to the image of King Henry VI which had the reputation of effecting miraculous cures.

p. 2. **Your father,** Sir William Paston, the judge.

p. 2. **Other day,** next day.

p. 2. **Anon,** a short time.

p. 2. **Garneys,** probably her godfather.

p. 2. **Emme,** uncle.

p. 2. **Play them,** amuse themselves.

p. 2. **Took,** brought to.

p. 2. **There,** where.

p. 3. **Your son.** This was probably Sir John Paston, born 1442.

LETTER III. **p. 3.** **Mote,** might.

p. 3. **With that,** on condition that.

p. 4. **Clepe,** call.

p. 4. **All that in them lyeth for you,** i.e. will labour for you as far as it lies in their power.

LETTER IV. **p. 4.** **Rewly,** grievous.

p. 4. **Undo,** undone.

p. 4. **But if,** unless.

p. 5. **Twenty nobles,** £6. 13s. 4d.

p. 5. **Owl.** This probably means "to deceive." To owl, was to be engaged in the illegal exportation of wool, and the work being carried on under cover of darkness to prevent detection the word probably came to have this derived meaning.

p. 5. **A letted,** have hindered.

p. 5. **Churtly,** angrily.

LETTER V. **p. 5.** **Con defend himself,** know how to defend himself.

p. 5. **Your father,** Sir William Paston, knight, died August, 1444.

p. 5. **Doles,** boundaries.

p. 6. **Hight,** called

p. 6. **Withset,** taken.

p. 6. **For,** because.

p. 6. **Purvey,** arrange.

p. 6. **Stansted Church,** in Suffolk, where Agnes Paston had possessions in the parish.

p. 6. **Tidings from beyond sea.** This refers to news of the giving up of Maine, truces, etc., on the marriage of the king (Henry VI) in the previous November.

LETTER VI. p. 7. **Half,** behalf.

p. 7. **Quyt,** requited.

p. 7. **Blackbeard or Whitebeard.** One of the common oaths of the time.

p. 7. **Demenys,** probably from the French *demence*, follies.

p. 7. **As in my chatel approving,** as is proved in my property.

p. 7. **Avail,** use, profit.

LETTER VII. p. 8. **Yeden,** went.

p. 8. **Myrr,** probably a murrain.

p. 8. **Assoil,** absolve.

LETTER VIII. p. 9. **The King's brother,** either Edmund, afterwards Earl of Richmond, father to Henry VII, or Jasper, Earl of Pembroke.

p. 9. **Device,** or ornament for the neck.

p. 9. **Beads,** necklace of beads.

p. 9. **Fresh,** gay or well-dressed.

LETTER IX. p. 10. **Chardeqweyns.** *Chare de quince,* a preserve made from the pulp of quinces. A "Book" of chardeqweyns was a measure weighing about 10 lbs.

p. 10. **Soulmass Day,** 2nd November.

LETTER X. p. 10. **Sadly,** seriously.

p. 11. **Yede,** went.

p. 11. **Dine.** It appears from this as though the dinner hour were between nine and ten in the morning.

p. 11. **Sydd,** sat.

p. 11. **Say,** tell.

p. 11. **Farcy,** a disease peculiar to horses, allied to glanders.

LETTER XI. p. 11. **Trussing coffer,** clothes chest.

p. 11. **Herring.** The herring and eels were for the Lenten food.

p. 11. **Bever,** liquor for drinking.

LETTER XII. **p. 12. Chevise,** provide.

p. 12. Ponyngs, frequently spelt Poynings.

p. 12. Twenty marks, £13. 6s. 8d.

p. 12. Wardship. The statute of Wardship was abolished in the reign of Charles II.

p. 13. Beadswoman, or beadsman was a person who prayed for another, in return for favours granted. Cf. the Beadsman in Keats's " Eve of St Agnes."

LETTER XIII. **p. 13. Endeavour,** duty.

p. 14. Lever, rather.

p. 14. Raised, have a new nap put on them.

p. 14. Musterdevelers, a kind of mixed grey woollen cloth.

p. 14. To do make me, to get made for me.

p. 14. The noble, 6s. 8d.

LETTER XIV. **p. 14. Wyndacs,** windlasses with which the bow-string is drawn home.

p. 14. Quarrel, an arrow with a square head.

p. 15. Plancher, floor.

p. 15. Cheap, bargain.

LETTER XV. **p. 15. Hele,** health.

p. 16. Basset, embassy.

p. 16. Ships of forecastle were the largest ships at that time, carrying about 150 men.

p. 16. Carvel was a medium sized ship.

p. 16. Spynne, a pinnace, carrying about 25 men.

LETTER XVI. **p. 17. Dormants,** beams.

p. 17. Cowntewery, counter or desk to write at.

p. 18. Be for to do, is to be done.

LETTER XVII. **p. 18. Yeoman of his ewry,** an officer who had charge of the table linen, etc.

p. 19. Elianor, Duchess of Norfolk, wife of John Mowbray, Duke of Norfolk, was sister of Henry Bouchier, Earl of Essex. Both she and her husband are buried at Thetford.

LETTER XVIII. **p. 20. Nerles,** nevertheless

LETTER XIX. **p. 20. Saint Margaret's Mass**, 20th July.

p. 20. Paper is deynty, choice, scarce. This letter is written upon a piece which is nearly square, with a portion cut out before the letter was written.

LETTER XX. **p. 21. Sey**, saw.

p. 21. My Lady of York, Cecily, Duchess of York, widow of Richard Plantagenet, Duke of York, and mother of Edward IV.

LETTER XXI. **p. 22. Worsted** is a small market-town in the east of Norfolk, formerly famous for the manufacture of the material of the same name.

p. 22. Happe me, wrap me up warm.

p. 22. Male, trunk. This and the following lines give us an example of John Paston's letter-writing in the form of verse.

p. 22. He shall Christ's hour, etc., the meaning of this line seems obscure.

p. 22. Good gill, agreeable companion.

LETTER XXII. **p. 23. Payd**, appayed, content.

p. 23. Ware, beware, guard.

p. 23. And, than.

p. 23. But, unless.

p. 24. Jape, deceive.

p. 24. Apeyer, grow worse.

LETTER XXIII. **p. 25. And**, if.

p. 25. My brother, Sir John Paston.

p. 25. My sister Anne, Anne Paston, afterwards wife of William Yelverton.

p. 25. Among while ye abide, during your abode.

p. 25. My sister Margery. Margery Paston, who afterwards married Richard Calle.

LETTER XXIV. **p. 25. Geane**, Genoa.

p. 26. Wryghe, twisted.

p. 26. Krott. The meaning of this is doubtful, but it probably means a *piece*.

LETTER XXV. **p. 26. My Lord of Gloucester**, afterwards Richard III.

p. 26. My Lord Archbishop, George Neville, Archbishop of York, brother to the Earl of Warwick (the kingmaker).

p. 26. Fallen, become.

p. 26. Meny, household.

p. 26. Disparbled, dispersed.

p. 27. A daughter, Elizabeth, afterwards wife of Henry VII.

LETTER XXVI. **p. 27. Rode again him,** rode to meet him.

p. 28. The Moor, a seat of the Archbishop's in Hertfordshire.

p. 28. Ebesham was a transcriber of books.

LETTER XXVII. **p. 28. Creancer,** creditor.

p. 28. The figs and raisins were for his Lenten food.

p. 29. Desired, invited.

p. 29. Otherwise than I was worthy, beyond what I was worthy of.

LETTER XXVIII. **p. 30. Hele,** health.

p. 30. My Lady Margaret, Margaret Plantagenet, sister of Edward IV.

p. 31. The Duke, Charles the Bold, Duke of Burgundy.

LETTER XXIX. **p. 32. Waxeth high,** grows tall.

LETTER XXX. **p. 33. Inforcing,** strengthening.

p. 33. Sad, serious.

p. 33. Copschotyn, cupshotten, apt to get a little drunk.

p. 33. Much upon, much like.

p. 34. Tackling, undertaking.

p. 34. Flower, probably his device or cognizance.

LETTER XXXI. **p. 34. The King,** Edward IV.

LETTER XXXIII. **p. 36. Greenwax.** Estreats which were delivered to the sheriff of a county from the Exchequer, bearing the seal of that court made in green wax, were therefore called "green-wax."

p. 36. Beware, lay out.

p. 36. Saint Agas day, Saint Agatha's day.

LETTER XXXIV. **p. 37. Ordain,** order for.

p. 37. And yet, even though.

LETTER XXXV. **p. 37. Quarter wages.** It seems from this that it was the custom for those in the king's service to receive the pay, both for themselves and their men, quarterly from the Exchequer.

p. 37. My lady, the Duchess of Norfolk.

p. 38. Let, hindrance.

LETTER XXXVI. **p. 39. My father,** John Paston, was buried in the priory church at Bromholm.

p. 39. Brigg, bridge.

p. 39. Or as ye seem, or what seems good to you.

p. 39. Earl of Pembroke, Jasper Tudor, half brother to Henry VI.

p. 39. Very, actual.

LETTER XXXVII. **p. 41. Delyverst,** nimblest.

LETTER XXXVIII. **p. 42. Queasy,** unsettled.

p. 42. Stiffler, stickler.

p. 42. Passagers, passage boats.

p. 42. My father, John Paston, imprisoned by Edward IV.

p. 43. Beset, bequeathed.

p. 43. And else, or else.

LETTER XXXIX. **p. 44. Rial,** a gold coin, worth ten shillings.

p. 44. Took him, gave him.

LETTER XL. **p. 45. Which is wont to be at border peraun-tys.** The meaning of this is probably " who is accustomed to be at the Border (of Calais) before this."

p. 45. Wend, thought.

p. 45. Quit them, acquitted themselves.

p. 45. Passage, passage boat.

p. 45. Ye may not make you wise in no wise. You must by no means seem to know anything of the business in hand.

p. 46. Aglets, pendent ornaments of metal.

p. 46. Neither not, neither note.

p. 46. Bill, a weapon having a concave blade and wooden handle, with sometimes a spike at the back. They seem to have been painted in different colours, or sometimes varnished.

p. 46. Glaze, polish.

LETTER XLI. **p. 46. Stomach**, resolution.

p. 47. Levest, dearest.

LETTER XLIII. **p. 49. Loader**, carrier.

p. 49. Puke, a dark colour, between black and russet.

p. 49. Done to weet, given to understand.

p. 49. Feel, sound.

LETTER XLIV. **p. 50. Wottys**, knows.

p. 50. For to be dead, for my life.

p. 50. Discur', discover.

LETTER XLV. **p. 51. By you afore**, from you before.

LETTER XLVI. **p. 52. Arayment**, apparel.

p. 52. She has never praised you too much, that is, though she has praised you, it is not more than you deserve.

LETTER XLVII. **p. 52. Sote**, sweet.

p. 53. By time, betimes.

LETTER XLVIII. **p. 54. £10 Flemish**, between £5 and £6 in English money.

p. 54. The emperor's son. Maximilian, son of the Emperor Frederick, married Mary, daughter of Charles the Bold, Duke of Burgundy.

p. 54. An hundred thousand ducats. A ducat of gold was worth about ten shillings. A ducat of silver, about five shillings.

LETTER XLIX. **p. 55. Ere than**, before.

p. 56. Bewared, expended in exchange.

LETTER LI. **p. 58. Incontinent**, immediately.

p. 58. Foodyd not forth, probably "footed," that is, has not set foot from his house.

LETTER LII. **p. 59. Breve**, to make up an account.

p. 59. Condeneth, give satisfaction.

LETTER LIII. **p. 60. The king's enemies be a-land.** This refers to the landing of Henry, Earl of Richmond, afterwards Henry VII, at Milford Haven.

p. 60. Bury. Bury St Edmunds, in Suffolk.

p. 60. Jackets of my livery. This shows that the royal troops were uniformed in the liveries of their respective lords.

p. 60. Norfolk. The Duke of Norfolk was killed at the battle of Bosworth, in August, 1485, not many days after the writing of this letter.

LETTER LIV. **p. 60.** This letter is from the Princess Elizabeth, sister to the king, Edward IV. She married John de la Pole, Duke of Suffolk.

p. 60. Lord Chamberlain, Lord Hastings.

LETTER LV. **p. 61. Easy,** little.

p. 61. For lack of acquitation. In the original "aqweytacon." It probably means that he has not acquitted himself well, or possibly "acquaintance."

p. 61. Lewd, uncouth.

LETTER LVI. **p. 62.** This library catalogue was written on a piece of paper about 17 inches long. One end became damp and the words are in some places obliterated. All the books, with one exception, are in manuscript.

p. 62. Cypio, Scipio.

p. 63. By letter, alphabetically.

Printed in the United States
By Bookmasters